LEAP OF REASON

LEAP OF REASON

MANAGING TO OUTCOMES
IN AN ERA OF SCARCITY

Mario Morino

With essays by Carol Thompson Cole; Lynn Taliento, Jonathan Law, and Laura Callanan; Isaac Castillo; David E. K. Hunter; Tynesia Boyea Robinson; Kristin Anderson Moore, Karen Walker, and David Murphey; Patricia Brantley; and Ethan D. Schafer

Edited by Lowell Weiss and Cheryl Collins

VENTURE PHILANTHROPY PARTNERS
IN PARTNERSHIP WITH McKINSEY & COMPANY

ISBN: 978-0-9834920-0-9

Library of Congress number: 2011926055

For additional copies of this book, please visit leapofreason.org.

Venture Philanthropy Partners
1201 15th Street, NW, Suite 510
Washington, DC 20005
vppartners.org

DEDICATION

To those leaders who made Venture Philanthropy Partners' first decade a broadly shared success: our generous investor families and institutions; our exemplary nonprofit partners; our wise board and advisors; our devoted team; and the many friends who provided invaluable insights along the way.

Your leaps of faith and reason have enabled disciplined investments in remarkable nonprofit leaders and have created outsize impact on the lives of children and families.

Contents

Author's Note

Extremely wise mentors, advisors, and friends, as well as a serendipitous stream of remarkable learning opportunities spanning more than five decades, built the foundation for this monograph and the message it seeks to convey.

I began my career in technology doing grunt work for a great General Motors team that computerized inventory control and manufacturing-cost accounting. Stints at Eaton Manufacturing, the U.S. Navy, and U.S. Time Sharing followed, providing me with rich learning opportunities and great "teachers." The practical wisdom and experience I gained served as vital building blocks for the foundational knowledge I have been so fortunate to aggregate. My deepest thanks to the many colleagues and friends of this era who helped shape my early years in the field.

A fortuitous meeting with **William L. Witzel** in 1972 was a seminal moment that led to many positive developments in my life, including this monograph's publication almost four decades later. Bill Witzel—affectionately known as Uncle Bill—and I co-founded Morino Associates, Inc., in 1973. The firm's success was based on a performance-management system that enabled Global 500 enterprises to manage and deploy their information technology resources—vast complexes of hardware, software, telecom, systems, and human capital. While our competitors focused on the technical intricacies of measurement, we, in large part thanks to Bill, focused on how executives could use this information to manage and to be more effective. I like to think we provided the context, judgment, and systems to translate these highly technical metrics into usable information. Uncle Bill, an unparalleled master in information and management discipline, is also responsible for my ingrained habit of asking "why?" before diving into the details of "what" or "how." The tried-and-true principles he modeled in word and deed were invaluable during my corporate days. They have also provided a priceless context for my work in learning how nonprofits can use outcomes, metrics, and information to be better at what they do.

Steve Denning and his team at General Atlantic, LLC, took a big leap of faith (with the benefit of hindsight, I suppose it could be called a leap of reason) in 1983 when they invested in Morino Associates. In the years that followed, they forever changed my definitions of "strategic" and "discerning." General Atlantic's approach of providing growth capital and strategic assistance in a culture of excellence to leaders and their organizations distinguishes them among venture capital and private equity firms. Their example profoundly shaped almost every aspect of my work and is at the very core of the Venture Philanthropy Partners (VPP) investment model. I am blessed that Steve remains an invaluable advisor and friend.

My transition from private- to social-sector thinking was influenced by so many wonderful minds that naming them individually would require hundreds of pages. But six people I am proud to call friends had the biggest influence on my thinking about outcomes, as well as the danger of unintended outcomes, in the social sector: **Michael Bailin**, **Charito Kruvant**, **Gary Mulhair**, **Billy Shore**, **Ed Skloot**, and **Bob Templin**. They shared their in-depth knowledge and keen insights to help me learn, course-correct when I strayed, and push my thinking.

I'm equally indebted to every stakeholder, past and present, at VPP. **Carol Thompson Cole** (VPP's exemplary leader), **Steve Seleznow**, and **Les Silverman** deserve special credit for their unwavering commitment to clarity of purpose and making a meaningful, measurable difference in people's lives. VPP has been on a learning journey through its investments in highly promising nonprofits that improve the lives of children and youth from low-income families. With each passing year, the organization has developed a clearer understanding of the importance of focusing on outcomes for greater impact and the challenges of establishing performance-management systems that work.

All of us at VPP, especially me, have benefited in myriad ways from our longstanding strategic partnership with McKinsey & Company. Their support of this monograph is simply the latest example. **Lynn Taliento** in particular has been a stalwart advisor who is never afraid to ask hard questions or provide unvarnished views. Every leader needs someone like her.

Along with Carol and Lynn, **Jonathan Law**, **Laura Callanan**, **Isaac Castillo**, **David Hunter**, **Tynesia Boyea Robinson**, **Kristin Moore**, **Karen Walker**, **David Murphey**, **Patricia Brantley**, and **Ethan Schafer** greatly enriched this monograph with their evidence-based insights and pragmatic examples, which give life to complex, challenging concepts. **David Hunter** and **Kristin Moore** deserve special recognition. No conversations about social outcomes, performance-management systems, "theories of change," or "logic models" are complete for me until David and Kris weigh in. In David's case, I am particularly grateful for the candid feedback and suggestions he so thoughtfully, and sometimes provocatively, provided since the outset of the monograph's development.

I am grateful to a diverse and talented group of individuals who graciously made time in their incredibly busy schedules to help us sharpen and improve the content of this monograph, including **Bob Boisture**, **Elizabeth Boris**, **Peter Goldberg**, **Harry Hatry**, **Darin McKeever**, **Fred Miller**, **Matt Miller**, **Amy Main Morgenstern**, **Nancy Osgood**, **Denielle Sachs**, **Lou Salza**, **Gene Steuerle**, **Nan Stone**, **Tom Tierney**, and **Mary Winkler**.

Lowell Weiss, **Cheryl Collins**, and **Victoria Vrana** played invaluable roles in shaping the monograph's content and form.

Lowell's abundant editorial talents, critical-thinking skills, and sharp insights, bolstered by his constant encouragement and wonderful sensitivity, made this monograph a reality. His commitment to purpose and quality raised the bar for all of us. Cheryl, my support anchor for almost two decades, is my source of institutional knowledge, serves as my noodge and conscience at Morino Ventures, and brings excellent writing, editing, and research skills to any project. Victoria played an invaluable role as reviewer, strategist, and coordinator. They are consummate professionals, highly respected colleagues, and even more important, close friends.

My thanks to **Chris Wright**, who produced this monograph's clean, professional look and feel, and **Katya Rice**, our copyeditor. The Morino Ventures team provides the platform for our philanthropic work and behind-the-scenes support that is vital and unheralded.

Dana, my life partner and spouse, and our three children—**Matthew**, **Rachele**, and **Nicole**—bring great happiness and purpose to my life, and their encouragement and love are cornerstones for anything I am able to achieve.

Though my name is on the cover, I am keenly aware that this volume would not have been possible without the work of so many individuals who have stayed the course with me over the years. I am incredibly grateful and privileged to have you in my life.

Foreword

by Carol Thompson Cole

―――――

Mario Morino, co-founder of Venture Philanthropy Partners, is many things to many people. Visionary entrepreneur. All-hours emailer. Demanding manager. Passionate advocate. Caring friend.

I see him, first and foremost, as a voracious learner.

Here's a classic example: When Mario retired from the software industry in 1992, he embarked on an eighteen-month listening and learning journey. He crisscrossed the country to visit with nearly seven hundred people in all walks of life—from nuns and schoolteachers to CEOs and senators. He had no set agenda for these meetings. His only goal was to glean insights on how he could most usefully and effectively apply his resources to helping children and families living in low-income communities like the one in southeast Cleveland where he grew up.

We at Venture Philanthropy Partners (VPP) are proud to publish this monograph with our longstanding strategic partner McKinsey & Company because it represents not only the learning Mario has done since that journey but also a host of highly relevant insights from his decades of work helping Global 500 companies manage their information technology resources for improved outcomes.

I encouraged Mario to write this monograph when I saw what a chord he struck in a series of four columns he wrote last year for *VPPNews* on the somewhat dry topic of assessment of social outcomes. I knew that his perspectives would have value for our investors and the nonprofit leaders we are privileged to support. But I had no idea that Mario's blunt, unminced words would tap into a deep well of frustration throughout the nonprofit sector with just about every aspect of the dialogue on social outcomes. His clarion call resonated with nonprofit leaders who haven't been able to find a shred of support from funders for collecting and using information to manage to outcomes. It resonated equally with funders who have had it with nonprofits that have no means whatsoever for determining whether they're doing what they say they do.

It should come as no surprise that VPP's investment partnerships and expertise in this field have provided a rich vein of insights for this monograph. It should also come as no surprise that we invited leaders directly and indirectly connected to VPP—Isaac Castillo from the Latin American Youth Center, Tynesia Boyea Robinson from Year Up, Pat Brantley from Friendship Public Charter School, Kris Moore and colleagues from Child Trends, David Hunter from Hunter Consulting, and Ethan Schafer from the Lawrence School—to enrich this monograph with lessons they learned on the front lines.

VPP has always made it a point to support those leaders who are both brave, committed visionaries and also introspective learners. Over time, through missteps and victories (big and small in both cases), we at VPP have gotten better at understanding how we can do more to help these leaders make the difficult cultural transition from simply having a genuine interest in improvement to truly infusing outcomes thinking into the way they manage their organizations.

Because if we've learned anything, it's that it does take *more* to support this difficult change. In our first portfolio of investments (2001 to 2009), we devoted a full 10 percent of our direct investments and countless hours of our senior leadership's time to helping our investment partners alter their culture and develop the human and IT systems necessary for managing to outcomes. And yet that big commitment was neither big enough nor early enough in our relationships.

With the help of a comprehensive outside analysis of our first-portfolio investments, we saw that five out of our twelve investment partners achieved the kind of transformative, systemic culture change we were hoping to spark. In our current fund, we aspire to produce an even higher ratio.

We're putting increasing emphasis on investing in leaders who already embrace the value of great information, even if they haven't yet had the external support to build systems for collecting and using information. In fact, in our new youthCONNECT initiative, we've asked all applicants to demonstrate a predisposition for using information to guide their operations. We're also providing longer-term funding, with a clear expectation that it will take at least two to three years of intensive work to create a true outcomes-focused culture. And we're learning to be more flexible in how we support this work. We've learned that we cannot impose our support for this type of change process, that we have to give our partners the time and space to do it their way, not our way. It's not going to stick if they don't own the process and the resulting systems.

And when it does stick—as it has for investment partners like the See Forever Foundation, Latin American Youth Center, Friendship Public Charter School, College Summit, Year Up, KIPP DC, and others—it truly helps nonprofits do a better job of meeting their missions. We consistently hear how much our investment partners value the strategic assistance we provide to help them become more focused and disciplined in managing their organizations, in a way that enables them to get started on the path toward managing to outcomes. In fact, the investment partners who experienced systemic culture change perceived that this support was one of the biggest external drivers of their results. "We have far better infrastructure [now]," one anonymous investment partner told our external reviewers. "Now we can look at how our programs can be strengthened for outcomes.... This has become part of our culture."

These investment partners report that during this time of very tight budgets, the time-consuming, expensive work of clarifying and assessing outcomes becomes more—not less—valuable to them. When resources are scarce, funders are more likely to ask for measurable results. But far more important, the nonprofit leaders themselves are eager for clarity on where to place their bets and how they can create the biggest impact for children and families.

We at VPP and McKinsey hope that after reading these essays you will come to share the view that managing to outcomes is far from a luxury. As Mario and our expert contributors make clear, we believe managing to outcomes is a necessity for any mission-focused organization that wants to create meaningful, measurable, sustainable change for those it serves.

If you're ready for this type of learning and cultural journey, we hope you'll use this book as a travel guide. In this slim volume we haven't been able to cover everything you need to know, but we think we can give you a reasonable lay of the land, help you get a good start on your itinerary, and spark good conversations for you and your travel companions—your staff, your board, and other key stakeholders.

And to help us on *our* learning journey, we of course welcome your feedback.

Bon voyage.

Introduction

by Lynn Taliento, Jonathan Law, and Laura Callanan
McKinsey & Company

———

Several years ago, Friendship Public Charter School, which manages ten schools in Baltimore and the Nation's Capital, developed some tools and processes for collecting data on students, teachers, and the schools as a whole. They built time into the academic calendar for reviewing the data and understanding their implications. And perhaps most important, the schools' leaders shared a deep commitment to using the data and the assessments to improve student outcomes.

With all of this in place—the data, the tools, the commitment—Friendship appeared to be a model nonprofit when it came to performance management. Yet Friendship's leaders realized they needed to improve. Because Friendship is accountable to many different stakeholders, they tracked an excess of metrics, overwhelming many staff members. The data they collected were not always explicitly linked to the outcomes they sought. Review processes for teachers and administrative staff were ad hoc rather than systematic. In short, Friendship had the foundations for performance management but lacked a coherent strategy for bringing it all together.

As you will read in more detail in the essays by Mario Morino (p. 1) and Friendship COO Patricia Brantley (p. 117), Friendship took the difficult steps necessary to build on its early experiences and create a world-class performance-management system. We were fortunate to partner with Friendship on this journey, and we were able to see firsthand—as we have with many other clients—the power that results from managing smartly against the right outcomes.

Today, Friendship is, by any measure, a high-performing organization. Its use of the performance-management system enables Friendship to make its already great teachers even better, helps principals do their jobs better, and provides board members with the information they need for more-effective oversight. All of which has had a discernible effect on Friendship's bottom line—helping students succeed.

It would be great if the story of Friendship were the norm; unfortunately, it's an outlier. Not many nonprofits manage to outcomes, and among those that do, few do it well. For that reason, *Leap of Reason* is an important contribution, and McKinsey is proud to partner with Venture Philanthropy Partners (VPP) to bring this volume to thousands of leaders who are predisposed to manage rigorously and effectively but can use a little encouragement and support.

The need for assessment and performance management seems obvious. So why doesn't every nonprofit define its goals, measure how it's doing, and manage accordingly? Not for lack of commitment to causes and communities. Not for lack of smarts. What seems to be missing is a combination of resolve to take on the hard work that change entails and, even more important, the appropriate resources to do so effectively. But as you will see throughout *Leap of Reason*, when leaders summon the resolve and resources, the results are worth the hard work.

Making Assessment Work

Through our work in the sector, we've identified five best practices for doing assessment well, doing it efficiently, and doing it sustainably. Given the alignment of our thinking and that of VPP, it should come as no surprise that all of these practices are fleshed out in greater detail in Mario's essay and the other essays that make up this important volume.

1. Hear the constituent voice. In order to get a complete picture of how and to what extent programs are delivering social impact, nonprofits must learn what the relevant constituents—the individuals and communities served by the program—have to say. Involving constituents in the design and implementation of an organization's ongoing assessment efforts, and in the interpretation of the results, helps ensure that a nonprofit is measuring what's relevant and valuable for them. And once the results are in, it's important to share the results with all stakeholders, as Patricia Brantley describes in her essay.

2. Assess to learn and do. Successful nonprofit organizations make learning the primary goal of their assessment. They begin by collecting as much information as they can about the target problem and the possible solutions. This way, they come to understand how their programs work and how they can work better. They also integrate assessment goals and results into all of their program decisions. In other words, assessment plans and program strategies are built hand in hand. Assessment is not just an academic review or an isolated exercise; it serves as a guide for the nonprofit's actions.

3. Apply rigor within reason. Understanding the true efficacy of a nonprofit also means periodically undertaking a more holistic program evaluation. Such evaluations complement the ongoing effort to manage to outcomes by verifying that regular results are in fact meaningful. When these evaluations are conducted, rigor is a desirable goal, but the most rigorous assessment approaches are not always feasible or appropriate. For example, randomized controlled trials are excellent when demonstrating the efficacy of a program prior to scaling. They are often less applicable, though, for new programs early in their life cycle.

Funders are notorious for requiring overly rigorous assessments. The result is a misallocation of resources and unnecessary headaches for the nonprofit. We've observed that the right level of rigor is the result of an open dialogue between nonprofits and their funders. By getting clarity on a program's strategic and assessment objectives, they can determine the level of rigor that's required.

4. Be practical—there's no need to do everything. Once nonprofits buy into the need to manage to outcomes, they sometimes fall into the trap of trying to measure everything. Developing a thoughtful, comprehensive assessment plan that is based on the right questions and crafted with funder participation avoids unnecessary burdens and expense. Moreover, many assessment tools already exist in the social sector. Successful nonprofits can tap into this trove and leverage such tools to great effect.

5. Create a learning culture. Robust assessment capabilities alone do not drive impact for nonprofits. From our experience, these capabilities must exist within a "learning culture" to derive the most value from assessment. Such a culture values honest appraisal, open dissent, and constructive feedback. It promotes intelligent risk-taking in pursuit of both insight and impact. It considers the relevant context of an assessment and makes difficult decisions based on evidence—even if that means ending a program.

Risks and Rewards

These practices can help nonprofits get assessment right. But to get assessment started, we must face up to a fundamental tension: The first time they conduct a rigorous assessment, nonprofits stand to lose as much as they might gain. Should their results provide evidence of significant impact, securing resources for their operations will be easier. However, poor results or—even worse—a misinterpretation of results could very well lead to lower levels of financial support, and even de-funding. At a minimum, stringent performance management will most likely mean changes in staff.

In short, the transition to outcomes-oriented management will almost certainly have some negative near-term implications for the organization. These changes, though, will just as certainly have a positive impact for the nonprofit in the long run as it becomes more effective in achieving its mission.

When done right, performance management is good value for the money. McKinsey has quantified the value of rigorous performance management in the private sector. Using data from our proprietary Organizational Performance Profile survey, involving more than 115,000 individuals in 231 organizations, we looked at whether strong organizational performance—including performance management—translates into financial results. The findings were clear: A company that measures in the top rather than the bottom quartile of organizational performance is more than twice as likely to attain above-average margins for its industry.

And then we went further, seeking to understand which specific attributes of organizational effectiveness were correlated with financial success. Once again, the findings were compelling. Robust performance management had the highest correlation with superior financial performance. Indeed, performance management beat out other important organizational attributes like innovation, capability, and environment. Companies with top-quartile performance in practices such as the consistent use of targets and metrics were 2.7 times as likely to financially outperform the median than those in the bottom quartile. Such data have convinced us that performance management is a no-brainer. It drives overwhelmingly positive results.

If the promise of such value for the money is not enough of a motivator, how else can nonprofits be convinced to adopt managing to outcomes? For starters, a sector-wide embrace of the learning mindset would help nonprofits and their funders make decisions in a positive, forward-thinking manner. For example, instead of simply de-funding an underperforming program based on a superficial understanding of results, a learning-centered approach would seek to understand the causes for failure and build upon that knowledge in future initiatives.

More radical steps could also compel nonprofits to embrace change. For instance, imagine an independent organization being created to certify whether nonprofits are adequately conducting assessments. Such a body would not be developing or conducting the actual assessment for nonprofits; this responsibility would remain with the organizations themselves. Instead, the certification agency would simply ensure that nonprofits are assessing themselves and publish its findings. For example, the body could determine whether the nonprofit has defined its outcomes and metrics that align with these outcomes, whether these outcomes and metrics are consistent with best practices in the relevant field, and whether the organization has at least basic systems for tracking these metrics over time. We raise this idea not necessarily to advocate for it but to push the thinking as to what might be possible.

Tailwinds for Assessment

Mission effectiveness will become an increasingly urgent issue in the decade ahead. To begin with, funders have come under immense fiscal pressures as a result of the deep recession we are only now emerging from. State governments across the nation are projecting budget gaps of $125 billion in 2012, according to the Center on Budget and Policy Priorities. Other sources of funding for nonprofits have also been declining: In 2009, donations to the nation's biggest charities dropped by 11 percent, according to an analysis by the *Chronicle of Philanthropy*. In such an environment, funders and donors will be forced to choose where and how to cut. They will undoubtedly demand more evidence of effectiveness from grantees as they make their difficult decisions.

Another trend is the emergence of impact investing. Investors who are actively seeking not only financial but also social or environmental returns want proof that their capital is delivering on all fronts. This trend is putting pressure on social enterprises both to show impact and to augment that impact in the future. Such pressure will certainly translate into spillover effects for the broader social sector.

These tailwinds suggest that assessment and managing to outcomes will become more widespread in the near future. Eventually, this discipline will become the norm. For all the rational fear of the inevitable challenges ahead, Mario's monograph and the accompanying essays in this volume should provide comfort that managing to outcomes is eminently doable. *Leap of Reason* also demonstrates that managing to outcomes is eminently *desirable.*

And not just for funders. For social sector leaders, the great benefit of managing to outcomes is that it gives them powerful new tools for learning over time, making better-informed decisions, and becoming more effective at what they are so passionate about doing. The greatest dividends of all of course accrue to the communities, the families, and the individuals with whom we work. They benefit from stronger schools, smarter clinics, and safer communities—all because of nonprofits' commitment to becoming better.

When you find a unique opportunity to make a real difference, you focus on it and constantly reassess results. This is discipline.

—Peter F. Drucker

Greatness is not a function of circumstance. Greatness, it turns out, is largely a matter of conscious choice, and discipline.

—Jim Collins

CHAPTER 1

We're Lost But Making Good Time

For the entire sixteen years I've been working full-time in the social sector, a problem has been gnawing at me, sometimes literally keeping me up at night.

Here's the problem in a nutshell: **We don't manage to outcomes, thus greatly diminishing our collective impact.**

Despite all the right intentions, the vast majority of nonprofits do not have the benefit of good information and tools to determine where they're headed, chart a logical course, and course-correct when they're off. They're navigating with little more than intuition and anecdotes. Only a fortunate few have a reliable way to know whether they're doing meaningful, measurable good for those they serve.

I know "manage to outcomes" may sound to some like fuzzy jargon—and frankly, I wish I had a better term. But I assure you, this problem is more than just a sleep-stealing concern of pointy-headed funders like me. It's a huge problem—and a huge potential opportunity—for the nonprofits themselves, for the families they aspire to benefit, and for society as a whole.

The problem is not new, but it is growing in urgency.

The cold reality is that in our present era of unsustainable debts and deficits, our nation simply will not be able to justify huge subsidies for social-sector activities and entities without more assurance that they're on track to realize results. Public funders—and eventually private funders as well—will migrate away from organizations with stirring stories alone, toward well-managed organizations that can also demonstrate meaningful, lasting impact.

To add more urgency, it's entirely possible that the bar may go even higher than that. Eventually public and private funders will see the value in favoring not just individual organizations that can demonstrate their impact but organizations working together in disciplined ways toward *collective* impact. As John Kania and Mark Kramer show in a thought-provoking article in the *Stanford Innovation Review* (Winter 2011), organizations working to achieve common outcomes within a broad, coordinated network—not just in their own silos—are much better equipped to solve big societal problems.

This monograph is intended for leaders who are willing to embrace the challenge of rigor head on, individually and collectively. It's for those who know in their bones that they want and need better information in order to fulfill the mission that compelled them to dedicate their lives to serving others.

Of course not every insight here will apply to every organization. No one would expect, for example, that small organizations with budgets under $1 million a year would invest hundreds of thousands or millions of dollars in building fancy performance-management systems to monitor results in real time.

But even the smallest organizations can find ideas here to help them manage in a way that allows them to know whether they're making a difference or not. I believe that's a reasonable minimum requirement for anyone who aspires to do good, applies for charitable status from the IRS, and asks others to commit their money or time.

Why Managing to Outcomes Is Rare

It sounds so simple, so basic. So why do so few nonprofit profession-als manage to outcomes despite a genuine passion for achieving a mission?

One big reason is that nonprofit leaders, even those who run the largest organizations, are not encouraged or supported to manage well. Many were "knighted" into their leadership positions because of their commitment to mission and achievements in serving others; they had no formal management training. Many heads of schools, for example, will share some version of the following lament: "I'm an educator, and I had no idea what managing was." Even in a sector blessed with truly remarkable leaders and visionaries, we do not rec-ognize and reward good management, and we have an acute shortage of management talent.

A second, related reason is that funders generally don't provide the kind of financial support that nonprofits need in order to make the leap to managing to outcomes. The truth, ugly as it may seem, is that nonprofit behavior is very much a function of what funders require. By and large, funders want to help nonprofits do the right thing. But far too many donors—big and small, public and private— have been conditioned to insist that every dollar go to "support the cause" through funding for programs. They don't want "overhead" to dilute their donations.

Unfortunately, this understandable desire to be careful about costs can deeply undermine the pursuit of impact. Yes, we have all seen some nonprofits that have unjustifiably high overhead costs, such as those that put on lavish galas that barely break even. But if funders see all overhead as wasteful, they will miss a huge opportu-nity to help their grantees make the leap to managing to outcomes— which, in my view, is the clearest pathway to impact.

To make the leap to managing to outcomes, nonprofits need cre-ative funders willing to think big with them—not just pester them for more information on results. They need funders who understand that making the leap requires more than program funding, and more than the typical "capacity-building" grant. They need funders who are willing to make multi-year investments in helping nonprofit leaders strengthen their management muscle and rigor.

Another reason nonprofits fail to manage to outcomes is that they fear that funders will use any information nonprofits collect against them, instead of using it to help nonprofits grow and improve. For example, educators often worry that school districts use student test scores and other educational data to restrict funding and fire teachers rather than to guide efforts to improve teacher and program quality for better student outcomes.

Granted, some nonprofit leaders have overcome these and other hurdles, and they have made truly meaningful progress toward improving outcomes by collecting, analyzing, and using information. Select hospitals like the Cleveland Clinic and the Mayo Clinic, for example, have made great strides in creating a culture of information-based introspection that allows them to use and apply the information they need on an ongoing basis. The same can be said for innovative human-service and education nonprofits such as Nurse-Family Partnership, Youth Villages, Harlem Children's Zone, Friendship Public Charter School, and the Latin American Youth Center, all of which are seeing positive early indicators of greater impact. And, fortunately, there are pioneers in the foundation world, such as the Edna McConnell Clark Foundation, that have lent their financial and strategic support to help their grantees manage to outcomes.

It's also true that a good number of nonprofits have come to appreciate the value of experimental and quasi-experimental evaluations, often conducted by third parties, to assess the effectiveness of specific programs. But even among these nonprofits, few have come to understand the importance of continuous, rigorous collection and use of information for guiding the management of their organization. This ongoing, management-oriented data collection and analysis is what managing to outcomes requires. It is a way for leaders and nonprofits to learn and grow. It is essential for achieving lasting impact.

Because of the impediments, far too few nonprofits even bother trying to manage to outcomes.

Among those who *do* try, far too many are missing the forest for the trees. They focus more heavily on the mechanics of measurement than on understanding what the data reveal. As a result, they are squandering precious time and financial resources.

Even worse, I've witnessed some misguided efforts—often foisted on nonprofits by funders—that have produced unintended negative consequences that go beyond the waste of money. In these cases, funders have turned assessment into an exercise focused on cold numbers—the equivalent of Robert McNamara's simplistic and terribly misleading Vietnam body counts—rather than using it to help nonprofit leaders achieve lasting impact for those they serve. These efforts are worse than no effort at all!

The Hudson Institute's eloquent and insightful William Schambra shares my concern about ill-considered, often harmful demands from funders. If nonprofits could speak truth to powerful foundations, he imagines they would say, "Let's decide jointly on a simple, coherent, user-friendly system to which we can both pay attention, which will prevail over bureaucratic [requirements] ... and which will feed into a serious body of knowledge. But until then, stop pretending that the problem is our lack of acceptable performance, rather than your lack of serious purpose."

"To What End?"

The simple question that has served me best throughout my business and nonprofit careers is "To what end?" I try to return to these three little words constantly during the life of any project or initiative, especially when I fear I'm drifting away from my original purpose or I'm starting to confuse ends and means.

I fear that when it comes to outcomes assessment, we have failed to keep our eyes fixed on the ends we are trying to advance.

In the wise words of David Hunter, managing partner of Hunter Consulting and a former director of assessment for the Edna

McConnell Clark Foundation, "The mess you describe indeed is enormous and very destructive.... Few people involved in this work have thought deeply about managing toward outcomes. Most put the cart before the horse—focusing on *how* to measure rather than on *why* measure and *what* to measure."

Every ounce of our effort on assessing social outcomes should be with one end in mind: helping nonprofits deliver greater benefits to those they serve.

Unfortunately, greater benefits are not the focus today. Measurement has become an end in itself.

- If greater benefits were the end, we would be working to help nonprofits clarify the results (outcomes) they are trying to achieve.

- If greater benefits were the end, we would do much more to help nonprofits collect and use the information that could best help them navigate toward those outcomes.

- If greater benefits were the end, we would properly differentiate between operational performance and organizational effectiveness. What good is it to focus on an organization's overhead costs or fund development levels if we don't have a clue as to how effective the organization is at creating benefits for those it serves?

- If greater benefits were the end, we would own up to how much encouragement and support nonprofits need in order to define and assess what they do and how well they do it. We've approached this challenge as if it's about numbers when it's really about having the right culture, a theme I will return to in detail in Chapter 3. Shifting the culture requires large and persistent investments of time, talent, and money.

Common Sense Left Behind

A vivid illustration of measurement run amok comes to us courtesy of No Child Left Behind.

I've had the opportunity to be engaged in K-12 education through Venture Philanthropy Partners' work with schools in the National Capital Region, through my participation on a number of national educational initiatives, as an advisor to leaders in education, through my deep engagement with a school in Cleveland for bright students who learn differently, and as a parent of three children. Based on these varied experiences, I, like many others, believe that the good intentions of the No Child Left Behind Act have led schools and students astray.

Of course I believe we need ways to judge our schools and to assess how well our students are doing. But No Child Left Behind does these things poorly. It is the classic example of metrics over mission.

The current regime of "memorization and testing" and the growing battery of standardized tests risk rewarding targeted test preparation while not informing us or the students themselves whether they are developing the relevant skills and competencies they and our society so sorely need. Yes, it's very important to achieve—and measure—core competencies like reading and math. But where are the incentives for schools to educate young people to be curious, engaged citizens capable of critical thinking and problem solving? Where are the incentives to encourage collaborative learning? Where are the incentives to nurture students' social-psychological development? Where are the incentives to give students practical experience in the ways of life outside of school?

A good friend and mentor who is a nationally recognized education leader sheds more light on this dilemma. He points to the work of Yale professor Seymour Sarason, who wrote as early as the 1960s about his fear of reductionist exercises that look at only one or two parts of what an organization does and then draw conclusions based on whatever is sampled. My friend notes, "Sampling may work fine for determining what's going on in someone's blood. But at school

7

these days [the only things we're sampling] are reading and math test scores, because they are easy to acquire and report."

Another friend and colleague, head of a high school for boys, shared similar concerns. He believes that a singular focus on standardized tests encourages schools to educate students as if they were widgets on a manufacturing conveyor belt rather than individuals with their own strengths, interests, and needs. (For insights on how schools can get beyond simplistic assessments, please see Ethan D. Schafer's essay on p. 127.)

Too Hard on "Soft" Outcomes

"To what end?" are three powerful words. But as I learned in my Catholic upbringing, two words that carry just as much power are "mea culpa."

Here's an example of how I looked too narrowly at outcomes—and, as a result, risked knocking nonprofits off mission.

In the early years of Venture Philanthropy Partners (VPP), we got a lot of resistance to my push for clearly defined outcomes from leaders whose organizations placed a premium on being holistic with their services and functioning as "community builders." Although I agreed with them in concept, I felt that a focus on "community building" was too soft to be a legitimate outcome. Outcomes related to "community building" are, after all, radically ambiguous compared with outcomes like reduction in teenage pregnancy and substance abuse.

I now see that serving the entire family (holistic services) and building community are some of the very things that create the kind of environment that allows youth to avoid risks, get an education, and prepare for jobs and college. I'm kicking myself for not having seen this earlier—because I *lived* this as a kid in the 1950s. I grew up in a technically poor neighborhood in Cleveland that was actually a truly connected and supportive community, a place where it was hard to fall through the cracks.

BASIC DEFINITIONS

Theory of Change—how we effect change

The overarching set of formal relationships presumed to exist for a defined population, the intended outcomes that are the focus of the organization's work, and the logic model for producing the intended outcomes. A theory of change should be meaningful to stakeholders, plausible in that it conforms to common sense, doable with available resources, and measurable.

Logic Model—what we do and how

The logically related parts of a program, showing the links between program objectives, program activities (efforts applied coherently and reliably over a sustained time), and expected program outcomes. A logic model makes clear who will be served, what should be accomplished, and specifically how it will be done (i.e., written cause-and-effect statements for a given program design).

Inputs—what resources are committed

The resources—money, time, staff, expertise, methods, and facilities—that an organization commits to a program to produce the intended outputs, outcomes, and impact.

Outputs—what we count

The volume of a program's actions, such as products created or delivered, number of people served, and activities and services carried out.

Outcomes—what we wish to achieve

Socially meaningful changes for those served by a program, generally defined in terms of expected changes in knowledge, skills, attitudes, behavior, condition, or status. These changes should be measured, be monitored as part of an organization's work, link directly to the efforts of the program, and serve as the basis for accountability.

Indicators—what we use to stay on course

Specific, observable, and measurable characteristics, actions, or conditions that demonstrate whether a desired change has happened toward the intended outcome. Also called "outcome indicators" or "predictive indicators."

Impact—what we aim to effect

To slightly oversimplify, the results that can be directly attributed to the outcomes of a given program or collective of programs, as determined by evaluations that are capable of factoring out (at a high level of statistical probability) other explanations for how these results came to be.

Editorial Note: These definitions were adapted from the Glossary of Terms *of the Shaping Outcomes Initiative of the Institute of Museum and Library Services, Indiana University and Purdue University Indianapolis;* The Nonprofit Outcomes Toolbox: A Complete Guide to Program Effectiveness, Performance Measurement, and Results *by Robert Penna; and the* Framework for Managing Programme Performance Information *of the South African government. The definitions were informed by distinguished reviewers who provided valuable insights.*

My friends and I benefited from a wide range of holistic services delivered by caring adults—from family to teachers to coaches and neighbors—who simply wouldn't let us fail. Of course we didn't know it at the time, but we were the focus of a reasonably well-coordinated network of providers that collectively produced an impact greater than the sum of good individual parts.

And yet when VPP investment partners talked about "community building," that sounded too intangible, not readily measurable—and, candidly, difficult to sell to our own stakeholders.

I regret not having been more open in my thinking back then. Instead of pushing back on what we were hearing, my colleagues and I should have done more to understand "soft" achievements that may in fact be every bit as real and important as "hard" outcomes. I aspire to do a better job of making them part and parcel of future efforts to assess outcomes and performance, even if that means using qualitative and/or subjective indicators.

The point is this: When public or private funders establish performance metrics and tie rewards or consequences to organizations' capacity to meet them, organizations and people will migrate to the behaviors that will allow them to meet their defined targets. If the metrics are appropriate and closely tied to mission, the organization can benefit. But if the metrics are simplistic and unmoored from mission, organizations will go racing in the wrong direction. To paraphrase Yogi Berra, they'll get lost, but they'll be making good time.

Backseat Driving

Ultimately, the benefits of an outcomes orientation must accrue to the nonprofit. Sadly, today most of the discussions of outcomes are being driven by funders demanding "more information on results" and not paying attention to what nonprofit leaders need in order to produce results.

We funders, in the name of "measurement" and "accountability," are foisting unfunded, often simplistic, self-serving mandates on our grantees—rather than helping them define, create, and use the information they need to be disciplined managers. In the words of Tris Lumley, head of strategy for the London-based New Philanthropy Capital, "Great organizations ... are built around great data. Data that [allow] them to understand the needs they address, what activities are likely to best address these needs, what actually happens as a result of these activities, and how to allocate resources and tweak what they do for even greater impact. Too often, funders set the agenda with their own requirements [and] cripple the organizations they're trying to help."

I strongly urge funders to see that assessment is most valuable if it is driven by the nonprofit itself. Attempts to define outcomes seldom produce positive results when they are imposed on organizations from the outside. The nonprofit needs to own the process and be the primary beneficiary of it.

And when we funders come to the table to encourage nonprofits to develop an outcomes orientation, we must be reasonable in what we expect. We can't expect a three-person nonprofit serving homeless girls to implement a robust information system. We can, however, encourage the nonprofit to define the outcomes it seeks to achieve for the girls it serves and to develop a clear picture of how its activities will help achieve these outcomes. And yes, even this type of tiny nonprofit can collect basic data to inform its work.

No matter how small the organization, we must not run away from outcomes and their measurement altogether—that is, do nothing to assess whether we are delivering on our promises to the families who turn to us for services. As David Hunter says, "It is a really, really bad thing for nonprofits to promise to help people improve their lives and prospects ... and then, when the matter is looked at closely, it turns out that they aren't doing that at all!"

Take-Homes in Tweets

 The vast majority of nonprofits have no reliable way to know whether they're on track to deliver what they promise to those they serve.

Managing to outcomes means investing in continuous collection and use of information to guide the organization's decisions and operations.

Managing to outcomes requires a significant culture shift within an organization. It is primarily about culture and people—not numbers.

Some funders have turned assessment into an exercise focused on cold numbers rather than using it to help nonprofits improve.

We must focus on *why* measure and on *what* to measure—not just on *how* to measure.

The nonprofit needs to drive the outcomes-assessment process and be the primary beneficiary of it.

Reasonableness and common sense must guide the investment in assessment.

CHAPTER 2

Innovation From the Periphery

Our sector needs a major reset on the approach to outcomes—from how we think about them to how we assess them.

More than anything else, our sector needs a singular focus on managing to outcomes for greater impact. This means encouraging and supporting nonprofits to do the following:

- Gain clarity, through thoughtful introspection, on what change they are trying to create

- Gain specificity on how they will accomplish that change

- Determine what information (hard and soft) will be most helpful for gauging whether they are on course to achieve that change

- Collect and use this information to plan, make important decisions, track, course-correct, and improve

- Combine all of the above with good judgment and keen discernment, which are more important than any single metric.

In my experience, some nonprofit leaders inherently think in terms of outcomes or are at least open to doing so. They bring more than intuition and personal agenda; they think deeply about the what, how, and why of their services; they are evidence-based; and they talk naturally and frequently about the change happening in the lives of their clients and beneficiaries. These leaders are genuinely hungry for reliable information to assess their value to those they serve. They *want* to manage to outcomes.

Leaders who have an innate desire for good information that's aligned with their mission are the ones most likely to develop a true performance culture and make a real difference in the lives of those they serve. And before those of you who rebel against the term "performance culture" get too incensed, let me urge you to step back from the jargon and debates of the times and ask yourself, How could individuals who serve others not want to know how they are doing and be able to share these findings with those they serve? This is what I seek to convey when I use the term "performance culture."

As I touched on in Chapter 1, using information to manage to outcomes and having a performance culture are dependent on an attitude and mindset that *must* come from within. Trying to impose this orientation on leaders and organizations is as constructive as trying to foist change on your spouse. As my better half will tell you (with a resigned sigh), it ain't gonna happen.

If you feel you have the mindset and tenacity to lead the transition to managing to outcomes, please be sure to read the "Ideas Into Action" section, which starts on p. 63. It contains a simple framework and questions to help you spark the right conversations within your organization and its board.

What Managing to Outcomes Looks Like

In this chapter I will describe a number of truly impressive innovators who demonstrate what is possible when organizations begin managing to outcomes.

Let me acknowledge first that I haven't done full justice to their innovative work—simply because words are not as good as pictures for illustrating what this work looks like in practice. I recommend that you visit savingphilanthropy.org, a site where you can see managing to outcomes in action. The site features clips from the one-hour documentary *Saving Philanthropy: Resources to Results*. The film, produced in conjunction with PBS by the brother-and-sister filmmakers Robby and Kate Robinson, is aligned with the themes of this monograph and coincidentally includes a few comments from me and several other contributors to this monograph, among them David Hunter and Isaac Castillo. It profiles social service organizations that have built outcomes-oriented cultures, and it highlights the role that forward-thinking funders play in the process.

Before he was featured in the provocative movie *Waiting for "Superman,"* Geoff Canada, founder and CEO of Harlem Children's Zone (HCZ) and one of my heroes, raised a stir with comments in the New York publication *City Limits*. When Canada was asked to define success for HCZ, he said, "The only benchmark of success is college graduation. That's the only one: How many kids you got in college, how many kids you got out."

Canada could not have been clearer on the ultimate outcome HCZ is focused on achieving. It's not improving reading levels. It's not getting kids to graduate from high school. It's not helping kids get into college. To Canada, these are important interim indicators that HCZ is moving in the right direction, but, ultimately, what matters is ensuring that those young people make it through college—because ample evidence shows that making it through college is what leads to lifelong results for the young people HCZ serves.

With that great clarity as a starting point, Canada and his team, aided by the Edna McConnell Clark Foundation, Bridgespan, and others, have gotten good at identifying the information they need to collect in order to manage to this outcome. Are all the kids in HCZ graduating from college? Of course not. But HCZ is on a very promising path.

Given that *Waiting for "Superman"* director Davis Guggenheim essentially held up Canada as a superhero, it is no surprise that HCZ came under greater scrutiny following the release of the documentary. For example, in a *New York Times* article entitled "Lauded Harlem Schools Have Their Own Problems," Sharon Otterman reported on criticism in education circles of the high per-pupil costs at HCZ schools (around $16,000 per year plus thousands more in out-of-classroom spending).

This criticism misses the point—and is representative of the kind of thinking we need to resist if we want to stay focused on the ultimate ends we're trying to achieve. Canada's mission is not merely to raise test scores. It is, in Canada's words, to "save a community and its kids all at the same time." And folks, that ain't cheap. The University of Pennsylvania's Center for High Impact Philanthropy has it exactly right: "Despite high costs of this particular model, the potential savings to society are huge. Considering costs in isolation tells you nothing about return on investment."

Another well-known managing-to-outcomes success story is Youth Villages, which helps emotionally troubled children through a wide range of residential- and community-based treatment programs in eleven states. Youth Villages rigorously tracks all the children it serves, during their treatment and often for two years after their discharge. "The state ... shouldn't be buying beds," says CEO Pat Lawler. "They should buy outcomes, successful outcomes."

Positive Outliers Close to Home

HCZ and Youth Villages have gotten an enormous amount of national attention for their efforts. But they are far from the only organizations that understand the value of managing to outcomes. This past year I had an opportunity to participate in demonstrations of three systems for managing to outcomes that were implemented by organizations I know well. All three of the systems, which the experts call "performance-management systems," encourage and reward curiosity and continuous exploration of how to do things better.

The first of these systems was created by an organization of which I am trustee: the nonprofit Cleveland Clinic. In brief, the clinic has developed a system that gives administrators and clinicians powerful and easy-to-use tools for making smart administrative and patient-focused healthcare decisions. Using this platform, the clinic recently started sharing data with a consortium of 256 hospitals.

The system feeds off the data from the clinic's repository of electronic medical records and is augmented with an array of other well-thought-out quantitative and qualitative data—from information on patient experience to data on blood utilization. The system has allowed the clinic to improve patient access; new patients now wait, on average, fewer than seven days to see a provider. It has also allowed the clinic to decrease its use of packed red blood cells by 10 percent, which has produced significant cost savings. These are but two examples of how this information is leading to better care and lower costs.

The other two systems were equally impressive—especially because they were developed by community-based organizations that are nowhere near the sheer size and scope of a world-renowned medical institution like the Cleveland Clinic.

One was developed by the Latin American Youth Center (LAYC), a VPP investment partner that provides a broad range of human services to help youth and their families live, work, and study with dignity, hope, and joy. At VPP, we have watched LAYC make significant progress in adopting an outcomes orientation, take material steps toward managing to outcomes, and initiate an evaluation approach that could lead to earning distinction as an "evidence-based program." LAYC's work in outcomes measurement and program evaluation has improved dramatically over the past five years. Today, LAYC is seen as a leader in the nonprofit community in the creation and implementation of data-collection systems, the use of data to evolve program design, and the generation of program-outcome information within a multi-service organization. (For more insights on LAYC's outcomes framework and performance-management system, please see Isaac Castillo's essay on p. 95.)

The other system was developed by Friendship Public Charter School, another VPP investment partner. In 1998, Friendship founder

Donald Hense and I stood in jeans outside a run-down DC elementary school. He pointed across the street and said, "That's where we're going to put our first school." Today, to Donald's great credit, Friendship is a thriving network of ten schools and academies, serving eight thousand children.

Friendship's performance-management system produces dashboards for each student, teacher, classroom, and school, providing timely qualitative and quantitative insights on how students are doing on the skills they need to learn. This information, easily available to all teachers as well as students and their families, allows for much earlier and more effective intervention when kids are having trouble. As word gets out about what Friendship has built, it will set a higher bar for schools around the country—including affluent private schools—and give a new sense of what's possible.

Angela Piccoli is a second-year teacher at one of the Friendship schools. This year her classroom included a majority of students who were low performers relative to their grade-level peers. "I was petrified to show students their data at the beginning of the school year, as many were barely readers," says Piccoli. "I thought it would unsettle the entire class and lead to overwhelming tension and anxiety." Sharing the data with students, however, is a non-negotiable requirement in Friendship's model and is expected of all teachers, so Piccoli did. And what happened? "My students responded to the data. They helped each other. They knew what they had to do and they kept improving. They have become cheerleaders who encourage each other."

Piccoli's students maintain their own graphs, which they color in with their results after each assessment. "I cried when I saw on my last interims how well the students did," she says. "It was the first time that they read the assessment themselves rather than having it read to them." Each of Piccoli's students has become a reader. And by taking ownership of their own data, the students have gained confidence in themselves as learners.

At the beginning of this year, Friendship added non-academic indicators—indicators related to students' well-being—to its performance-management system. According to Friendship COO Patricia Brantley, "We saw immediately the interrelationship between struggling teachers and struggling classrooms. Attendance and discipline issues weren't spread out evenly among classrooms; there was a clear correlation between student non-academic outcomes and teacher performance."

At Friendship's first meeting to share data on attendance and truancy disparities between classrooms, one principal remarked, "Kids can't just fall through the cracks anymore, because we can see them right when they need us to do so. This is the data that I needed to ensure that every adult is focused on the most important work." As Brantley puts it, "We use the data as the common driver of urgency for leadership and urgency for management." (For more insights on Friendship's performance-management system, please see Brantley's essay on p. 117.)

From Periphery to Core

All of the previous examples suggest that positive change is percolating. For even as most nonprofits and funders in the core of our sector continue to "major on minors," it's clear that some leaders are achieving remarkable progress on the periphery of our sector.

It is impossible to predict how quickly change will migrate from the periphery to the core. For some, change will be slow, especially for funders stuck in their ways and nonprofits that are woefully under-resourced or don't have a leader to champion outcomes thinking. For other funders and nonprofits, change will come sooner. This is especially true when they get a good look at the way the innovators on the periphery are managing to outcomes today and see the greater impact they're achieving as a result. To borrow from Hewlett Foundation CEO Paul Brest, those who get a glimpse of what's possible feel like sailors navigating by dead reckoning in a world with GPS.

This phenomenon brings back a lot of memories from my career in the software industry, when I had a front-row seat on the process of technology adoption and the systems change it enabled. Today I'm seeing a convergence of (a) a rather select group of nonprofit leaders hungry for information to help them do better what they do; (b) fundamental changes in technology, data architecture, and data accessibility; and (c) external financial pressure to demonstrate value for the money. This convergence is eerily familiar to those of us who worked with the likes of Boeing, the U.S. Department of Defense, and Federal Express in the 1970s, '80s, and '90s to implement early versions of performance-management systems.

In those days we helped executives peer into the ways that information systems could help them manage their resources and produce improved results (i.e., outcomes). And, gradually, as executives saw the potential with their own eyes and were able to put it into the context of their organizations, their view of what was possible with good information was forever changed.

In those business sectors, innovation migrated from the periphery to the core relatively quickly. Investors could see how performance-management systems contributed to companies' bottom line, and so they were willing to fund the hard work that went into building these systems. As I will discuss in greater detail in Chapter 5, in the social sector we need to make a similar case to funders. We need to prove that investments in managing to outcomes and performance-management systems will allow organizations to produce greater impact.

Mindset Over Matter

As we develop the case for investment in performance-management systems, it's vital for us to avoid getting caught up in a mere appreciation for the technologies they use or the aesthetics of their user interfaces. Take it from a former high-tech executive: Technology is *not* the decisive factor in whether organizations make the transition to managing to outcomes and raise their impact. Far more important is the mindset of the leaders who put these systems in place—a mind-set that can prevail even in organizations that can't afford to build sophisticated data systems.

Leaders like the ones I've profiled in this chapter take on the challenge of managing to outcomes not because it's "important," not because it's a trend or a good marketing tool, and not because a funder or investor said they had to. They do it because they believe it to be integral to ensuring material, measurable, and sustainable good for those they serve.

In the next chapter I will offer insights on how leaders can help to cultivate this mindset in their organizations through the two most powerful tools at their disposal: people and culture.

Take-Homes in Tweets

Funders can make a big impact on the causes they care about if they encourage and support their grantees to do the following:

Gain clarity on what change they are trying to create

Gain specificity on how they will accomplish that change

Determine what information will be most helpful for gauging whether they are on course

Collect and use this information as the basis for understanding what's working, planning, decision making, and improving.

Leaders with an innate desire for good information are the ones most likely to make a real difference in the lives of those they serve.

Leaders who see performance-management systems for the first time feel like sailors navigating by dead reckoning in a world with GPS.

The best performance-management systems help users do what they do better and make what they do easier.

The technology behind these systems is not nearly as important as the mindset of the leaders who put these systems in place.

CHAPTER 3

Culture Is the Key

In my forty-plus years of experience in the for-profit and nonprofit sectors, I have come to see that there's a common denominator among organizations that manage to outcomes successfully: They all have courageous leaders who foster a performance culture.

An organization's culture has a huge impact on whether the organization can achieve what it hopes to for those it serves. To me, all organizations should strive not only to foster a *healthy* culture, where their people understand the mission and feel appreciated for their role in fulfilling it. They should also strive to nurture a *performance* culture.

Once again, I use the term "performance culture" with some trepidation. I know it's radioactive for some, especially those in the education field.

But the term as I'm using it shouldn't be threatening. I mean simply that the organization should have the mindset to do what it does as well as it possibly can and continually seek to do even better. For example, there are many teachers I know who would not naturally see themselves as representing or contributing to a performance culture per se. And yet they stay after school to tutor or counsel; grade papers late into the night; care immensely about helping students learn and grow; and even show up to cheer their students on at games, plays, and other events. These teachers may not see what they do as being driven by a performance mentality, but their actions in serving their students speak louder than words.

A Great Culture Starts With Great People

Nurturing a performance culture begins with recruiting, developing, and retaining the talented professionals you need to fulfill your mission. Failure to do so is, to me, literally a dereliction of duty of board and management—from executive director to line supervisor. Board and management need to "get the right people on the bus, in the right seats," in the famous words of management expert Jim Collins.

I'm a big believer in the notion that what makes things happen is people. Best practices are wonderful, but they are most effective in the hands of highly talented people. I'd take the best talent over best practices and great plans any day of the week. Too many of us think that organizations and systems solve our challenges. They play a vital role, but the key lies in the people who execute those plans.

To amplify this point, I will share a long quotation from a leader of great distinction in the educational, philanthropic, and nonprofit sectors:

> I despair over the money being expended by our sector on evaluation, measurement, etc. The simple truth is that if you don't stay focused on the quality and energy of leadership, all the rest is beside the point. We all continue to avoid the tough but vital question of gauging ... the assessment of the human element.... My own experience that now stretches over fifty years is that we are a long way from quantifying the critical element of judgment.

So this is the basic question: Do you have the right talent, leadership, and judgment in place to execute your mission? Next to questioning the mission itself periodically, this is the most important question boards and management must ask themselves.

Asking and answering this "hot potato" question is difficult. It might require change and improvement on the part of those already on the bus, *including the person driving it*. It might require bringing different people on the bus. Most often it requires a combination of the two.

The truth is that we're not good at this type of change in our sector. We often sacrifice the quality of our programs and services in order to protect those who aren't doing their jobs well.

Why? For one thing, we generally lack effective ways to assess the performance of staff so that we can help them improve or move on. More important, executives just don't want to deal with the confrontation that's sometimes required when we know a staff member's performance isn't good enough. We avoid providing the honest, constructive feedback people need to improve. When steps for improvement don't work, we are loath to make changes, especially terminations, lest we rock the boat. Too many of us allow appeasement and accommodation to override doing our best for those we serve.

It's a delicate balance when you're dealing with someone's career (and livelihood). Candidly, there are times I've made the go/no-go call too quickly. I've seen people develop to become solid performers, even leaders in their organizations, after I thought they weren't going to make it. Fortunately, others saw something in them that warranted going the extra step.

Such decisions are never to be taken lightly, and there's no checklist of steps. It comes back to the quality of judgment of those making the decisions. Intuition and instincts are an important part of the equation.

In the early years of VPP, I took the team to visit the offices of General Atlantic, LLC, a preeminent global growth-equity firm that invests to build great companies. In a discussion with one of the best executives I've had the pleasure of knowing, one member of the VPP team asked, "What's the most important thing you do to help the firms in which you invest?" He said simply, "Make sure the firm has a great CEO, and then make sure he or she has or gets a great number two. It's all about the people."

I can't begin to relate how true this has been in all aspects of my business and nonprofit careers. In 1987–88, as CEO of Morino Associates, Inc., I recruited a new executive-management team with the background and experience to lead our firm to where we aspired to go. Trust me, it was not a popular action, but it proved central to allowing the firm to achieve what it did in the years that followed.

In 1989 we merged with another firm to create LEGENT Corporation. One of the smartest and best actions we took was to recruit three new outside board members who were seasoned executives and had "been there, done that." Absolutely priceless! Very soon I came to see that they had more insights in their little fingers about building great organizations than I possessed in my entire body (and I was heavier in those days). Being around them while we worked through the integration of the firms was invaluable professional development for me.

After I transitioned to the nonprofit world, recruiting Carol Thompson Cole to VPP in 2003 was a defining action. She both fit into and helped build our culture in positive ways. Carol's leadership is the primary factor underlying the broad-based acceptance and success of Venture Philanthropy Partners to date.

If we had more time and space, I could offer a dozen additional stories that emphatically illustrate the value of getting the right people with the right judgment at the right time to help an organization succeed. But what is probably even more instructive is to acknowledge that each time I strayed from going after the right leader, I inadvertently set my new hire up for failure and needlessly caused great angst for those around me and our organization. And it always took a toll on those we served.

Nurturing Culture Change

Leaders can't simply create by edict the organizational cultures they desire. The best we can do is to influence culture through our words and deeds. An organizational culture is a complex, organic system that has a lot in common with a coral reef. "Coral reefs are one of nature's most beautiful creations," says high-tech CEO Jim Roth. "Man has not figured out how to create them. What we do know is we can care for them and nurture them to survive and thrive or kill them through neglect and abuse." The same is true of culture.

So how, precisely, do we nurture a culture through words and deeds? What can we do to strengthen the connective tissue that binds an organization together and cultivate an orientation toward performance? Here are some of the things that I think are most pertinent:

○ **Recruit culture leaders.** An effective way to influence culture is to find people whose personalities, attitudes, values, and competencies exemplify the culture to which you hope to evolve. Sometimes these leaders are sitting right in your midst, waiting for the opening and encouragement to do their thing. At other times you have to recruit from outside the organization. It is often the combination of developing from within and recruiting from outside that fosters a performance culture.

○ **Walk the talk.** Model—that is, live—the behavior you want others to practice. In my corporate life that meant getting out to talk with and listen to our customers. It meant (and still does) little things like answering a phone within a few rings and picking up that piece of trash on the floor. And it meant bigger things, like being sure that the decisions on corporate direction and people's careers were grounded in the organization's guiding principles.

I've been fortunate to be involved in a three-year transformation of a school, guided by a leader the board recruited in 2007. From its inception, the school's teachers and staff genuinely cared for the students they served. In fact, this caring attitude was the defining characteristic of the school for more than two decades. But as the organization grew from a small school with several grades to nearly four hundred students in grades one through twelve across two campuses, the stakes changed.

Starting with the leader's unrelenting commitment to the students, intense work ethic, strong values, and abiding belief in the potential of his staff, he led a quest to change the culture. And he did so by first "walking the talk" himself and then getting the faculty and staff to do the same. For example, he, the faculty, and the administrative staff changed the dress codes for faculty; highlighted the importance of individual responsibility; ended the practice of students sometimes referring to teachers by first names; encouraged curiosity and new ideas; achieved a greater level of transparency; and made excellence in teaching the norm. They effectively modeled behaviors of a learning community for the students to emulate, and it's beginning to yield results.

○ **Know what you stand for.** Take the time to flesh out your core beliefs and your guiding principles, and then do what it takes to make them more than just slogans on the wall above the water cooler.

In my corporate life, I was a fanatic about customer service, and we recruited people we thought were inclined the same way. One day I dropped into the office of a systems developer who wanted to share a new idea. As he sketched his suggestions on a whiteboard, I asked him what our customers would think. He was utterly dismissive of our customers' input, and that turned out to be a career-altering error. Being highly responsive to and respectful of our customers was a guiding principle of our firm and a sacred part of our organizational culture.

A well-defined and accepted set of guiding principles is important to any organization, but I suspect that it is especially important for those in the nonprofit sector. It may sound corny, but take the time—through an inclusive process—to define the principles that guide what you do as an organization and as individuals. Then ensure that these principles are embraced by and instilled in every member of your team.

Northeast Ohio's Lawrence School, which is the subject of the essay by Ethan Schafer on p. 127, did an outstanding job in this regard. You can see the clarity of the school's vision, mission, and guiding principles on its website (lawrenceschool.org/about/mission). There's nothing pro forma about these statements. The leadership team—staff and board—invested three months in debating and fleshing them out. Once that comprehensive process was complete, every member of the leadership team took the time to assimilate these definitions and then work to instill them throughout the full faculty, administration, and student body. The definitions are no longer words on paper but principles upheld by everyone in the school.

○ **Answer the question "To what end?"** As I noted in Chapter 1, with all the rhetoric around mission, scaling, accountability, and the like, the reality is that we often have to go back to basics and ask, "To what end?" Defining an organization's true purpose is absolutely essential to cultivating a performance culture.

Some years back, I participated with a school's leadership team in a frustrating process that was supposedly about instilling "excellence in education." The school's programs were, at best, only average. Many within the ranks knew that the academic programs were middling, and some parents suspected it as well. As is always the case, the students knew it most of all. Yet the school's administrators and board members refused to face reality and failed to examine what they were trying to accomplish for the students they served. "To what end?" went completely unaddressed. The lack of clarity about purpose continually limited the leadership's ability to put the school on a trajectory toward excellence.

In contrast, I've had the recent opportunity to get to know a Catholic high school and its new leader. From our discussions it is evident that he has a clear vision for what excellence in education looks like for his institution—a vision that's deeply rooted in the institution's values. The leader is taking bold steps with his board to ratchet up the dialogue on excellence. He has already moved to introduce the International Baccalaureate (IB) program for the school's educational core and brought in a top-notch educator with extensive IB experience to implement it. Clearly, this school is setting a course to answer "To what end?" in a way that will provide strong guidance for faculty, students, and families.

○ **Ensure that everyone's moving toward the same destination.** In my business life we once brought in a speaker to inspire our team and get everyone on the same page. He gave great examples of getting folks involved and buying into mission, the normal song and dance of inspirational speakers. But he wrapped up the session with a pithy statement that is indelibly etched into my memory: "Catch the vision or catch the bus!" Harsh? For sure, and it's unlikely that you'll use it at your next all-hands meeting. On point? Very much so.

Don't get me wrong. I welcome constructive questioning, and many colleagues, past and present, have war stories about "spirited" debates that took place within our teams. But once the debate draws to a close and we set a plan of action, everyone is expected to close ranks and align to the overarching goals. It's even OK for the dissenters to continue their line of questioning within the team. But if their actions, overt and covert, work in direct opposition to the goals, that's the time when they need to move on.

Several years ago, an organization I know well undertook a transformation to address some problems and materially improve its programs and services. The organization had done a good job while it was small. As it expanded to provide a broader set of services, quality suffered. To rectify this, the organization's leaders decided to revamp what they did to be more evidence-based in their programs.

Some of the longtime staff members who were fixed in their ways found this new approach hard to accept, even though the changes were showing positive results. After a reasonable length of time had passed, the leaders set out to work with those not yet onboard, making it clear that the organization was committed to this new approach. The leaders laid out their expectations clearly and helped staff members transition to the new approach. This clarity and thoughtful approach resulted in the departure of some staff members, but those who chose to remain "caught the vision."

○ **Ensure a balance between leaders and managers.** Leaders are *inherently* disruptive, dissatisfied with the status quo, questioning. They move the organization and people out of their comfort zones. They drive change, always looking for ways to improve. An appropriate motto of leaders is "The only way you can coast is downhill!" A healthy organization needs leaders in key strategic positions—including, of course, the top!

Managers, by contrast, have to keep the trains running on time. They make sure people do their jobs well, achieve intended results, and have the competencies and resources they need to succeed in their work. An appropriate motto of managers is "Stay focused; hold steady on the tiller."

There must be balance. If leaders hold too much sway, the organizational culture often ends up being chaotic, even threatening, and the organization becomes at best unreliable. If managers prevail too much, the organizational culture tends to be self-satisfied and tied to maintaining the status quo. The organization will be a poor bet for sustained high performance.

○ **Be clear and direct about what you expect.** I've struggled for a long time to uphold this principle and still don't always do a very good job. Many years ago, my partner in the software business overheard me talking to a person on our development team. Never one to miss a chance to help me get better, my partner said, "You really raked John over the coals for not doing a good job on the routine you asked him to develop. Did you ever explain to him what 'good job' meant? If not, you have no grounds to criticize him. You never let him know in clear enough terms what you wanted from him—and then you expected him to read your mind!"

If you want associates to do their jobs as well as they can, you have to be clear about what you want them to do. You have to have a process for assessing their performance—one that involves their input—so that they get regular feedback on what they do well and where and how they need to improve. One of the tragedies of most organizations is that the people who work there get almost no meaningful feedback, robbing people of vital insights for how they could be better.

○ **Encourage self-improvement and personal growth.** Are you ever puzzled (or dismayed) when people don't ask others for advice or help? When there is an important discussion and people don't ask questions or take notes? When people aren't curious enough to explore beyond their assignment? When people don't give input?

A few years back I was working with school leaders to help them frame a business plan, and I vividly remember asking one of the principals, "What do you think about how we can improve the curriculum?" First came a long pause and a look of astonishment. Finally the principal replied, "No one ever asked me for my input before. We are simply told what to do." In my view, that was a crystal-clear sign of an unhealthy culture and an organization not likely to achieve its intended outcomes.

It is not just important but imperative to encourage personal growth. One nonprofit executive shared what he tells his people: "Life is change. Therefore, as individuals or as an organization, by definition, either we're getting better or we're getting worse."

In my experience, people who improve, innovate, and adapt are curious souls and self-learners. An organization's culture should encourage people to ask questions, seek advice, do research, improve what they do and how they do it, help each other, push each other's thinking, probe, nudge, adapt, look at things from different vantage points. All of these behaviors lead to improvement and innovation for the organization and the individuals who are part of it.

Conversely, if you really want to stifle this kind of positive culture, all you have to do is kill the dialogue by saying, "This is how we do things"; demean or punish people for asking questions or offering advice; fail to acknowledge when they need help or direction; or avoid being clear and forthright. You can be sure you'll turn everyone off. They'll keep their heads down and do only what's required of them. They'll comply to survive—and add nothing more.

My Darth Vader Years

I don't want to leave you with the impression that I've figured out all the mysteries of nurturing a performance culture. In fact, when I look back over my career, I see many things I would do differently—especially things I would do with more compassion. Those who know me will not be shocked to learn that back in 1991 at a raucous team celebration for our software business, I was presented with a humorous video depicting me as Darth Vader.

Despite my shortcomings as a leader, I worked very hard to nurture a performance culture. Factoring in that I might be engaging in slightly revisionist history, I believe that the people in the company really cared about what they did and how they did it. They cared about our customers and each other—so much so that these relationships often grew to close friendships, anchored in mutual respect. People worked hard not because I decreed that they should but because they wanted to do their work very well; they wanted to experience the exhilaration of excellence. When we made mistakes, our openness allowed us to quickly admit and rectify them. It was inherent in the culture that we would respond this way.

It wasn't always sunshine and lollipops, because there was always pressure to perform to high expectations—not just to the firm's expectations but to their peers' and their own. But I have received many notes over the years from those who worked with me during that era saying that those years were some of the most enjoyable and rewarding in their careers. And I honestly believe our work had a lasting impact on those we served (our customers) and the field.

I don't wish Darth Vader–style leadership on any organization. What I do wish is that all leaders would take the time to establish real clarity on the ends they want to achieve, have the courage to line up the right team to fulfill the mission, make clear what they expect of their teams, be disciplined in their execution, and model the behaviors they want the organization to exhibit. When you combine all of these things with a good heart, respect, and genuine caring, you almost inevitably shape an organizational culture in which people take pride in what they do and are eager to excel and play a role in fulfilling the organization's mission. And that's a great formula for creating a real difference in the lives of those you serve.

Take-Homes in Tweets

An organization's culture has a huge impact on whether the organization can achieve what it hopes to for those it serves.

All organizations that manage to outcomes successfully have courageous leaders who foster a performance culture.

An organization with a performance culture focuses on doing what it does as well as it can and continually seeks to do even better.

We can't simply create by edict the culture we desire. The best we can do is to influence culture through our words and deeds.

The best way to influence culture is to recruit and retain top talent whose values and skills match the culture to which you aspire.

Take the time to flesh out your guiding principles, and do what it takes to make them more than just slogans on the wall above the water cooler.

Ensure that everyone is moving toward the same destination. In other words, help people catch the vision or catch the bus.

CHAPTER 4

Incremental Change Is Not Enough

In the last chapter I shared ideas for how nonprofit leaders can drive culture change within their organizations to support a relentless focus on doing the most good for those they serve. In this chapter I want to look at driving this type of culture change at a sector level. As hard as it is to drive culture change at the organizational level, we have to set our sights even higher. As you will see in my unflinching forecast below, we will need nothing short of quantum, sector-wide change to accomplish our important missions in this new era of brutal austerity.

An Emerging Movement

Starting a century ago with the likes of Rockefeller and Carnegie, leaders have looked for ways to achieve greater impact by increasing the effectiveness of their work in the social sector. The past decade and a half has been particularly fertile for research, development, and dialogue on the topic of effectiveness.

Just look at some examples of what has emerged over the past fifteen years:

○ Bill and Melinda Gates and Warren Buffett roared onto the phil-anthropic scene with a willingness to invest massive resources based on data and evidence.

○ We witnessed the fundamental transformation of the Edna McConnell Clark Foundation toward evidence-based funding, culminating in the launch of the Growth Capital Aggregation Pilot. This pilot brought together foundations, corporations, and individual philanthropists to commit $120 million in growth capital to support the expansion of three highly effective organizations: Nurse-Family Partnership, Youth Villages, and Citizen Schools.

○ Large, well-established foundations such as Hewlett, Robert Wood Johnson, Irvine, Annie E. Casey, and Kellogg placed greater focus on nonprofit effectiveness and impact.

○ Many top-notch consultants and advisors that focus on effectiveness and impact got their start, including the Bridgespan Group, the McKinsey Social Sector Office, the Monitor Institute, FSG Social Impact Advisors, the Center for Effective Philanthropy, Grantmakers for Effective Organizations, and Arabella Philanthropic Investment Advisors.

○ VPP, New Profit, the New Schools Ventures Fund, Nonprofit Finance Fund Capital Partners, REDF, Robin Hood, SeaChange Capital Partners, Strategic Grant Partners, Social Venture Partners, and others ushered in a different way to help nonprofits succeed.

○ New Philanthropy Capital, Impetus Trust, The One Foundation, and the European Venture Philanthropy Association have helped spread the philanthropic-investment approach far beyond America's shores.

○ Outcomes theory and thinking gained greater intellectual heft thanks to the efforts of Michael Bailin, Elizabeth Boris, Isaac Castillo, Paul Decker, Harry Hatry, David Hunter, Kristin Moore,

Robert Penna, Elizabeth "Liz" Reisner, Lisbeth "Lee" Schorr, Nadya Shmavonian, Gary Walker, Karen Walker, Hal Williams, and others.

○ Donors Choose, GlobalGiving, GuideStar, Kiva, MyC4, Network for Good, Social Impact Exchange, VolunteerMatch, and scores of innovative online models have been changing the way people give their treasure and talent, as outlined in an outstanding report by Lucy Bernholz with Ed Skloot and Barry Varela (leapofreason.org/Bernholz).

○ Capital markets for social innovation are no longer a pipe dream, as anyone can see on vivid display at the annual SoCap conference in the Bay Area and in the work of pioneers like the Acumen Fund.

○ The President created the White House Office of Social Innovation and Civic Participation, and the Corporation for National and Community Service launched the Social Innovation Fund.

I'd *so* like to believe that this progress is a sign of a pervasive, disruptive transformation throughout the social sector. I'd like to believe that the majority of nonprofits are now poised to materially improve their impact by being more analytical about causal relationships and more rigorous in how they assess their performance. I'd like to believe that the majority of funders are poised to make decisions based on evidence and merit rather than loyalty, stories, and relationships. Yet the reality—in absolute terms—is that the promising developments I've highlighted here and in Chapter 2 still touch only a small minority of nonprofits, foundations, and donors.

Drucker's Prescient Challenge

A number of years ago I had the privilege of participating in a three-day "Social Entrepreneurs Initiative" hosted by the philanthropist Robert Buford and led by the legendary management expert Peter

Drucker. In the group of a dozen amazing participants, I was clearly the weak link—the one who would have been kicked off the island first if we'd been on reality TV.

Mr. Drucker, always prescient, saw the outlines of an emerging movement toward greater innovation, effectiveness, and impact in the social sector. Though impressed by the emerging movement this group epitomized, he wasn't convinced that it would amount to wholesale change in the mindset and culture of the social sector. The key was to figure out how to grow this emerging movement into a true force for change.

My fervent hope is that Managing to Outcomes could serve as the banner under which many of us with diverse skills, talents, and offerings could come together to meet Drucker's challenge and convert a promising movement into a potent force. And let me reiterate that the Managing to Outcomes banner is *not* about pushing nonprofits to drink the metrics Kool-Aid, implement fancy reporting technologies, or adopt complex measurement methodologies. It is about encouraging nonprofits and funders to cultivate for themselves an outcomes-focused mindset and the passion to be as effective as we possibly can for those we serve!

Neither VPP nor I have earned the place or have the chutzpah to lead a charge of this magnitude for the sector. But to help kick things off, I would welcome helping to convene a select group of early adopters, those leading practitioners who have "been there and done that"—especially those who overcame and learned from failures. It is my hope that out of this cadre of leaders and doers will emerge a collective leadership that could put our sector on a different and much more rapid trajectory.

The Big Game Changer

I don't like to sound Machiavellian, but the first order of business for this leadership group must be to heed the fifteenth-century philosopher's admonition to "never waste the opportunities offered by a good crisis." (No, Chicago mayor Rahm Emanuel was not the originator of this sentiment.) The crisis I'm referring to is the dire fiscal reality for federal, state, and local governments, which will have an impact on almost every nonprofit in America whether or not it receives government funds.

Our economy has taken a broadside hit, and most economists and budget watchers agree that we are now in the midst of a profound structural shift. Congress will eventually enact major cuts in the growth rates of Medicaid, Medicare, and Social Security. Even more threatening to our sector are likely cuts in the real amount of discretionary spending—not just growth rates. In a cruel irony, these cuts will not only reduce the supply of funding for many of the services that nonprofits provide; they will also dramatically increase the demand for these services.

The magnitude of the combined hit—greatly reduced funding and increased need—will require organizations to literally reinvent themselves. Incremental responses will be insufficient. I agree wholeheartedly with Dr. Carol Twigg, president and CEO of the National Center for Academic Transformation, who concludes, "We will have to produce significantly better outcomes at a declining per-unit cost of producing these outcomes, while demand for our services will be increasing."

I've consulted some of the country's smartest budget experts on these trends. They tell me that, if anything, I haven't gone far enough in my depiction of this stark reality. For example, they point to the dire situation at the state and local levels, which will only get worse when the federal government pulls back. As National Council of Nonprofits CEO Tim Delaney reported in the *Nonprofit Quarterly*, "State government revenues fell almost 31 percent in 2009, which is the sharpest decline since [the Census Bureau] started collecting such data in 1951.... State and local governments are starving."

The frightening budget forecasts at the federal, state, and local levels are just one manifestation of a larger philosophical shift. In the twentieth century, under Democrats and Republicans, government services expanded dramatically. Many of us took for granted that when we identified a new program to handle some unmet need, we could say to the government, "Now add that to your portfolio."

The reality today is that outside of healthcare, the expansion of public funding and government services as a share of our economy is going to come to an end, if it hasn't already. In this new era, public policy debates increasingly will focus on how best to use or repurpose existing resources.

To respond to such a daunting game changer, we will all need to raise our games to a much higher level and seize the opportunity in the crisis. As Education Secretary Arne Duncan spelled out in a speech he called "The New Normal," the challenge of doing more with less "can, and should be, embraced as an opportunity ... for improving the productivity of our education system ... if we are smart, innovative, courageous in rethinking the status quo." *New York Times* columnist David Brooks agrees: "This period of austerity will be a blessing if it spurs an effectiveness revolution."

And let's not forget that effective programs can reduce the nation's budget problems. For example, if serious and expensive problems like dropping out of school are prevented, then productivity and tax receipts will increase. Similarly, if criminal behavior is reduced, then taxpayers will benefit from lower costs for incarceration and rehabilitation.

We need to rethink, redesign, and reinvent the why, what, and how of our work in every arena from education to healthcare to public safety—as will the government. We need to reassess where we have the greatest needs so we can apply our limited resources to have the most meaningful impact. We need to be much clearer about our aspirations, more intentional in defining our approaches, more rigorous in gauging our progress, more willing to admit mistakes, more capable of quickly adapting and improving—all with an unrelenting focus and passion for improving lives.

It's no longer good enough to make the case that we're addressing *real needs*. We need to prove that we're making a *real difference*.

Real-Life Opportunity Costs

To illustrate the urgency, I will offer some examples of organizations that are *not* making a real difference—and that will inevitably come under greater scrutiny as funding choices become harder and harder.

Drug Abuse Resistance Education (D.A.R.E.), a drug-prevention program whose advertising bumper stickers are about as ubiquitous as McDonald's restaurants, is present in more than half of U.S. school districts, all fifty states, and thirteen foreign countries. Created in 1983 by then–Los Angeles police chief Daryl Gates, D.A.R.E. is typically delivered in schools by visiting police officers presenting the dangers of drug use. The program has gained enthusiastic support among educators, law enforcement agencies, and the media.

But there's a hitch: *Numerous studies have shown D.A.R.E. to be without impact. It simply does not measurably affect drug use.* There is an enormous social cost to this lack of results—the lost resources that could have been put into prevention programs that actually work, and the lost potential of children and young adults who might have been diverted from drug use by such programs.

Consider another well-known program, Scared Straight, which arranges for juveniles who are getting in trouble with the law to meet, up close and personal, lifers who let them know that prison is hell. The idea is that this will terrify the kids and propel them back onto the straight and narrow path.

But you might want to know that rigorous experimental research shows that *Scared Straight is more harmful to teens than doing nothing.* What does this mean? It means that Scared Straight has been proven to *increase violence* among teenagers who participate in its visits to prison. Nevertheless, Scared Straight not only thrives in the U.S. but has spread to at least six other countries. (Please see p. 96 for Isaac Castillo's candid account of how a program under his purview was exacerbating domestic violence rather than ameliorating it— and how his organization, informed by outcomes data, addressed the problem head-on.)

Unfortunately, we see examples like D.A.R.E. and Scared Straight in every community.

We see mentoring programs where frequent turnover among mentors and failed matches reinforce youngsters' sense of their low worth and poor prospects.

We see hospitals and clinics that provide grossly substandard care and do not follow the medical mantra of "Do no harm."

We see foster-care programs that stop supporting kids when they "age out" of the system at age eighteen or twenty-one—exactly when they need intensive support (50 percent will be homeless within a year).

We see programs aimed at getting people off welfare and into jobs that don't provide any job-based coaching and support—even though it's well known that job retention is a huge challenge for people leaving welfare.

I certainly don't mean to suggest that these programs typify the nonprofit sector. There are many demonstrably effective nonprofits that are playing vital roles in our communities and helping people improve their lives every day—not to mention countless others that may be making a difference but simply do not have the data to demonstrate their success. But the stark truth is that there are too many nonprofits that are just not doing enough to ensure that they're making a positive difference. I am truly frustrated by the number of cases I come across in which nonprofits settle for mediocrity or cause potential harm to those who have given their trust.

Perhaps I am so passionate about this issue because I've seen, up close, the real-life costs and consequences of ineffective programs. The academic development of a member of my extended family was set back several years by a school that, despite its worthy intentions, did not have the capabilities to meet this young person's needs. A dear friend died prematurely when a "healthcare provider" turned out to be a callous radiation butcher. Weeks before her death, she said, "I have every ground to sue him, but why? I'll be dead anyway."

If Not Now, When?

Keep in mind: You're hearing this frustration from a stalwart social-sector advocate. If I'm this frustrated, think about the mass of voters who do not have a strong understanding of the social sector and how they would react to radio, TV, and Internet pundits pointing an angry finger at a host of social programs that not only waste taxpayer money but might actually cause harm to purported beneficiaries. Imagine the Congressional hearings that would ensue. Imagine how hard it would be to defend, much less advance, all the good that our sector does. Imagine all the babies that would get thrown out with the bathwater.

Are we ready to take a sector-wide leap of reason? If not now, when?

Take-Homes in Tweets

The past decade and a half has been fertile for research, development, and dialogue on the topic of effectiveness.

Progress will be incremental, however, unless we grow this effectiveness movement into a true sector-wide force for change.

Our country's grim fiscal situation is both a frightening reality and an opportunity to make a quantum change.

There are already too many examples of ineffective programs that cast a bad light on our sector and will not fly in an era of austerity.

Imagine all the babies that will get thrown out with the bathwater if our sector *cannot* offer evidence that our work matters.

We must mobilize a sector-wide leap of reason. If not now, when?

CHAPTER 5

A *Quantum* Leap of Reason

Back in the 1980s, an authority in the field of change management shared his view that dramatic personal change doesn't happen until what you had stops or is taken away. The death of a loved one, a serious illness or health scare, job loss, divorce, or financial ruin—each of these is the sort of turning point he had in mind.

The social sector is in for a similar jolt over the next decade. We can respond with infighting, robbing Peter to pay Paul, or continuing our incremental efforts to be better. Or we can respond with greater discipline, unity, and focus on making a quantum change in the effectiveness and impact of our entire sector.

In this chapter, I will draw from the insights of key thought partners who believe deeply in the necessity of making a quantum change. Borrowing from their brainpower, I offer the beginnings of a brainstorm on one of the trajectories for sector-wide actions that could allow us to find the opportunity in crisis.

The ideas I will offer are not exhaustive. They are at best a collage of ideas to begin the conversation, stimulate more thought, and provoke rich debate. I hope they show that there are concrete, tangible actions catalytic leaders could take to help get this sector over the big hurdles that have blocked widespread adoption of outcomes thinking and practice.

Demonstrate What's Possible

A natural place to start is to help nonprofits and funders alike under-stand the "value proposition" for taking the leap of reason. Yes, our frightening budget realities provide a big incentive—the "stick"—for taking the leap. But we need to be intentional about making the "car-rot" element clear as well. We must shine a bright spotlight on the wonderful nonprofit innovators who are showing that managing to outcomes—driven by mission and applied with judgment and a sup-portive culture—is a pathway to much greater impact.

There are many different ways to show nonprofits and funders what they'll gain if they take the leap of reason. Matt Miller, the wise writer and thinker, suggests commissioning seasoned journalists to produce compelling magazine-style narratives that tell the story of nonprofits that have successfully made the leap of reason. Imagine the value of these narratives if they documented in plain English how managing to outcomes helped an organization produce greater impact, how continuous improvement became the new norm, how turnover diminished as staff members felt greater accomplishment, and how much easier it became to provide meaningful information to the board and funders. The articles, published quarterly, could serve as a launching pad for a series of convenings and webinars featuring the nonprofit leaders profiled, as well as policymakers, funders, and experts.

High-quality videos could extend the reach and persuasive power of these stories. We need videos with viral potential (e.g., the finalists in Tactical Philanthropy's Fantastic Video Contest). Perhaps it would make sense to commission short films from name-brand filmmakers like Davis Guggenheim and others who have worked closely with the philanthropist Jeff Skoll and his Participant Media or Ted Leonsis and his "filmanthropy" efforts.

Establish a Prestigious Award

The best awards do a good job of bringing positive attention and legitimacy to a field or discipline. The Nobel Memorial Prize in Economic Sciences is not an official Nobel Prize. It was established in 1968, nearly seven decades after the original Nobel Prizes in Physics, Chemistry, Physiology or Medicine, Literature, and Peace. Its creation gave the field of economics, which at the time was considered "a soft science" not nearly on par with a "hard science" like chemistry, a huge boost in intellectual credibility.

Given how much positive attention the MacArthur Fellowships (a.k.a. the "genius grants") generate each year, I suggest that the organizations that best exemplify managing to outcomes be awarded cash prizes of $500,000 each, the current MacArthur level. Prizes should be awarded to organizations within different size categories. The awards would highlight great successes for everyone to see, and the money would allow the winners to fuel further progress. And, to be consistent with the philosophy of outcomes assessment, we should follow up with the winners to see whether or not their successes continued, and why.

We ought to explore connecting these awards to Drucker's legacy. One way to do that would be to build on the Peter F. Drucker Award for Nonprofit Innovation, which goes to "existing programs that have made a difference in the lives of the people they serve." (I've had no discussions with the team at the Drucker Institute that administers these awards, so I have no idea if this is feasible.)

Create a Social-Sector Analogue to ISO 9001

In the business world, more than a million companies and organizations around the globe have embraced the ISO 9001 quality standards for their management systems. The standards are published by a Geneva-based NGO called the International Organization for Standardization (ISO).

It is important to note that certification is *purely voluntary*. So why have more than a million companies done so? One big reason is that companies have a direct financial incentive to adopt the standards: Many major purchasers require their suppliers to achieve certification so they can ensure that suppliers have management systems in place for delivering what they promise.

And there's another carrot for companies to adopt the standards: Research suggests that companies get a strong return on their investment in ISO 9001 certification. On average, those that receive certification do better financially and operationally than peers of similar size without certification.

The social sector would greatly benefit from a similar *voluntary* program of management standards, based on the core principles of managing to outcomes. If the management standards were thoughtfully developed and allowed for differences among nonprofits of different purposes, sizes, and budgets, these standards could proliferate throughout the social sector. Over time, public and private funders would most likely come to require their grantees to achieve certification, just as major corporate purchasers have done with their suppliers. Enlightened funders would provide funding for nonprofits to go through the certification process and to train staff in how to apply these practices—perhaps leveraging volunteers from corporations or government agencies with ISO standards experience.

For funders, there would be great value in knowing that prospective grantees adhere to outcomes-based management practices that give them a good chance at producing real impact. The value would be just as high, or perhaps higher, for the nonprofits themselves. Achieving certification would not only help nonprofits to accomplish more; it would also help nonprofits attract higher levels of funding, talent, and overall support.

Encourage Performance-Based Funding

For years we've heard discussions in our sector about "funding what works." Why not take this concept to the next level?

I had considerable experience with performance-based funding in my business career. Our clients often negotiated to put "service-level agreements" in place, for example. By the terms of the agreement, we had to meet clearly stated performance criteria in order for us to receive full payment for our services.

It's more challenging to enter into this type of agreement in the social sector, owing in part to the lack of systems for collecting and documenting performance metrics. But it can be done. At VPP we enter into agreements with our nonprofit investment partners that lay out mutually agreed-upon goals for organizational development actions, outputs, and outcomes. An after-school tutoring program's goals included (a) goals for strengthening the organization (actions), (b) goals for increasing the number of students receiving tutoring (outputs), and (c) goals for improving students' reading proficiency (outcomes). When done right, goals like these become a nonprofit's North Star.

We review our investment partners' progress against these goals on an annual basis. We are not overly rigid in these reviews; we recognize that the best-laid plans often go awry for reasons not within the nonprofit's control. But these reviews create common expectations, and they have a significant impact on the goals, structure, and size of our investments in subsequent years. VPP has good company in this type of funding. The Edna McConnell Clark Foundation, Robin Hood, New Profit, New Schools Ventures Fund, REDF, and other private funders tie their investments to performance criteria.

In this era of government scarcity, an increasing number of public funders are sure to adopt similar practices. The Urban Institute's *Making Results-Based Government Work* presents a comprehensive study for introducing performance management into all facets of state government to "link monetary rewards/penalties to achievement of the desired outcomes." At the federal level, President Obama has included $100 million in his 2012 budget proposal to test Social Impact Bonds, a concept imported from Great Britain. "The plan uses private, profit-motivated investment money to fund public services up-front," says *Fast Company* contributor Alex Goldmark. "The government only pays if the services deliver as promised, and only out of government cost savings. No taxpayer money wasted on failed pro-grams in this plan."

Performance-based funding can be as fancy as Social Impact Bonds or as basic as a relatively modest grant my family and I made to a school in Ohio several years ago. To develop the grant agree-ment, I worked with the school administrators to establish clarity on the results the school was after; what they planned to do (their logic model); and what specific criteria we would use to determine mutu-ally whether they were making progress and whether continued funding was warranted. The agreement, just three pages in length, made it easy for both parties to align expectations.

Build Sector Knowledge

Our sector must build and make accessible the knowledge base on managing to outcomes. The "Compendium of Top Readings" on page 77 is one attempt, but more comprehensive initiatives are under-way. Here are three that are particularly noteworthy:

- Child Trends, Social Solutions, and the Urban Institute are joining forces to build the Outcomes and Effective Practices Portal (OEPP), which will become available on the web in late 2011. Currently in beta testing, OEPP provides nonprofits in the human services field a set of comprehensive resources on program outcomes, effective practices, performance indicators, and tools for gauging performance. Ultimately, OEPP will help leaders answer critical questions like these: (a) What outcomes should I expect from my program? (b) How can I measure these outcomes in a valid but not overly onerous way? (c) What are the key components of my program that I should manage and track on a day-to-day basis to give it the best chance of achieving its intended outcomes?

- McKinsey & Company's Social Sector Office has an impressive repository it calls Learning for Social Impact (lsi.mckinsey.com).

The site includes tools, best practices, lessons learned, profiles, interviews, landscape analyses, and historical perspectives on outcomes assessment.

○ The Annie E. Casey Foundation's National Survey Indicators Database (tarc.aecf.org/initiatives/mc/mcid/) is designed to help users find survey questions, measures, and instruments that can contribute to meaningful data-collection activities.

Over time, these and other initiatives to build and disseminate knowledge will have to broaden to cover the entire landscape of social-sector programs. And they will have to get increasingly sophisticated about providing insights tailored to specific organizations at specific points in their development. After all, managing to outcomes never lends itself to a cookie-cutter, one-size-fits-all solution, as a notable leader in the social sector sagely cautions:

> *We can't treat all nonprofits as if they are the same, simply because they fall within the same IRS category. For instance, does managing to outcomes apply in the same way for a human services organization with a $75 million budget, of which 90 percent or more of its revenue comes from public sector contracts; a high school serving six hundred students with a $6 million budget, of which 80 percent is funded from tuition and 20 percent by charitable giving; and a community arts organization with a budget of $600,000 with more than 70 percent of its funding from private donations? ... Not only are the three organizations vastly different in their strategic responsibilities as well as their governing responsibilities; they are also widely different with respect to their operational capacities and staffing needs.*

In addition, I would also hope to see new low-cost, high-value networks and initiatives emerge. For example:

- **An Evidence and Outcomes Research Network.** This "expert network" would coalesce research expertise from the likes of Child Trends, Hunter Consulting, Public/Private Ventures, and other nonprofits, academic research centers, and research groups from federal labs and agencies. The network would be organized around major areas like disease management, early-childhood development, and workforce development. It would conduct or commission research—which would be peer-reviewed—to provide a more objective and systematic assessment of what works, how, and how well. (The Coalition for Evidence-Based Policy, which works to inform federal policy, is already showing the value of having a good clearinghouse of information on social programs and interventions that have the strongest evidence of effectiveness.)

- **A Managing-to-Outcomes Support Network.** This network would be a professional learning community that would enhance idea exchanges among practitioners, researchers, academics, and consultants. In addition to the informal learning that such networks make possible, they can help create structured services such as webinars, videocasts, and wikis. The managing-to-outcomes support network could use these services to systematically advance understanding of the intricacies of transitioning to a culture of outcomes assessment.

- **Managing-to-Outcomes "Boot Camps."** These boot camps would bring together small groups of nonprofit and funder executives for intensive three- to five-day workshops that would help them get started on the path toward managing to outcomes.

○ **Managing-to-Outcomes Fellowships.** Such fellowships would allow nonprofit leaders and senior staff to work within and learn from nonprofits with a well-established culture and systems for managing to outcomes.

○ **Certified Roster of Consultants.** A consultant roster would provide the names of individuals and organizations that are highly qualified to assist leaders who want to take the leap of reason or have already taken the leap and need support and guidance to be even more effective.

Develop Models for Outcomes-Driven Collaborations

When nonprofits gain greater clarity on the outcomes they seek to achieve, they often come to two realizations: "We can't get there from here" and "We can't get there alone." An increasing number of youth-development and education organizations, for example, are likely to conclude, like the Harlem Children's Zone, that (a) the outcome that ultimately matters most is the percentage of young adults who finish college or get a good job, and (b) moving the needle on this long-term outcome is beyond the reach of any single organization, no matter how good its programs.

Therefore, a focus on long-term outcomes should bring with it an inexorable pull toward multi-organization collaborations capable of delivering the comprehensive set of services and supports needed by those served. And that is why, as we develop a field-wide strategy to help individual nonprofits develop strong performance cultures, we also need to invest in learning how to build successful outcomes-driven collaborations.

Important work is already in progress. Cincinnati's Strive Partnership, profiled by John Kania and Mark Kramer in the *Stanford Social Innovation Review,* is focused on achieving better results in education, from cradle to career. The collaboration involves more than three hundred leaders of local organizations, including nonprofits, district schools, foundations, government agencies, universities, and community colleges. "These leaders realized that fixing one point on the educational continuum—such as better after-school programs—wouldn't make much difference unless all parts of the continuum improved at the same time," Kania and Kramer report. "Their ambitious mission became to coordinate improvements at *every* stage of a young person's life."

In the National Capital Region, youthCONNECT, a new public-private partnership led by VPP and supported, in part, by the Social Innovation Fund, has brought together six nonprofits into an outcomes-driven network to help guide young people aged fourteen to twenty-four to a successful adulthood.

Taking this concept to scale on a national level is Achieving the Dream: Community Colleges Count, a coalition of 130 community colleges representing 1.6 million students. The coalition is helping community colleges develop a sharper outcomes orientation by focusing all its members on tracking data to measure and improve student persistence and completion, which traditionally have been shockingly low, especially among minority and low-income students. Achieving the Dream teaches colleges how to use data to develop a culture of evidence, and it encourages courageous conversations about what the evidence reveals about student achievement.

These and other existing initiatives are the first small steps up a long, steep hill. It is hard enough for a single organization to build a performance culture. It will be far, far harder to build a network of organizations, each committed to building a performance culture and all animated by a shared commitment to outcomes-driven collaboration. But this is a hill we have to climb, for only such collaborations can achieve the social gains that we so urgently need.

Improve Voluntary Outcomes Reporting

In addition to supporting efforts to revise the IRS Form 990 to be a better reporting tool, we need to do much more to enable sites like GuideStar, the National Center for Charitable Statistics, Charity Navigator, Charity Guide, GiveWell, and GreatNonprofits to make performance data—not just operational and financial data—available on the nonprofits they profile.

I am not one who believes that more information automatically translates into better donor decisions. The truth is that giving is fiercely personal, often driven more by loyalty and emotion than by evidence. Having said this, I do believe that our fiscal crisis will force greater decision-making rigor on governments, with a powerful spillover effect for private funders.

In a changing world in which funders increasingly ask to see outcomes and impact information, the nonprofits that voluntarily share it would have a strong comparative advantage. The organizations that were not inclined to provide it would stand out for their lack of an outcomes culture and transparency.

Voluntary reporting of outcomes information need not be highly sophisticated to be valuable. For example, nonprofits could provide the following:

- Brief descriptions of their intended outcomes, their methodology for producing these outcomes, and an explanation of the length of time it might take to see results (given that, realistically speaking, few outcomes can be tied to an annual reporting schedule)

- The number of individuals they served for whom the outcomes were achieved as well as the number for which progress toward outcomes was made (moving the sector away from the nearly useless but widely accepted norm of "people touched")

- And, ideally, the estimated average cost to produce the intended outcomes.

An advisory board of distinguished experts could provide stewardship and help establish credibility for this reporting. A facilitated group of peer reviewers could assess the filings, reject those that are inadequate, and offer advice to those who pass and those who fail the review. Such an effort could easily be included as part of the social-sector ISO certification I sketched earlier.

Encourage Funders to Invest in Nonprofits' Management Capacity

I know many nonprofit leaders who are not managing to outcomes today but are strongly predisposed to do so. They inherently know what their outcomes are and very much want to assess and manage to them. But they are severely hamstrung by the lack of funding available to do this hard work.

As I touched on in Chapter 1, there is no escaping the fact that funders will have to provide the general operating support that nonprofits need to develop the talent as well as build the human processes and technology systems for managing to outcomes. At a minimum, funders should be supporting capacity-building efforts to help nonprofits (including executives and staff) to (a) track the outcomes of those served, (b) undertake at least basic analysis of this information, and (c) identify how they can use the information to learn and improve their programs over time.

For my money, these investments have a tremendous return on investment. They are anything but "pouring dollars into overhead"!

As Carol Thompson Cole noted in the Foreword, in its first portfolio VPP made direct investments of nearly $3 million (10 percent of its total investments) to support outcomes-oriented culture change and the development of performance-management systems. On top of that significant financial investment, our professional investment team and outcomes experts provided significant strategic assistance to support these efforts. VPP is investing even more to help its second portfolio of nonprofit investment partners manage to outcomes.

We Like Difficult

It is not clear to me whether the ideas I've laid out in this chapter have real merit. But I do know this: We must tap the collective brainpower of the social sector to get great ideas on the table now, ahead of the budget axe.

Addressing the fiscal challenge will not be easy. But that is no excuse for us to bury our heads in the sand.

A few years ago, Melinda Gates spoke before the Council on Foundations and shared a lovely, telling anecdote. She once overheard her youngest daughter, Phoebe, struggling to tie her shoes and saying to herself, "This is difficult. But I *like* difficult."

Melinda and her husband like difficult as well. Difficult is how they have chosen to give meaning to their lives.

Chuck Feeney is another remarkable philanthropist who likes difficult. After transferring virtually all of his personal and family assets to the Atlantic Foundation, he invested strategically and provided sterling moral leadership to overthrow a century of accepted dogma in favor of a new philosophy called "giving while living."

Today, "giving while living" is no longer just a clever slogan or an outlier concept. It has influenced and inspired a whole generation of donors, including Melinda and Bill Gates.

I believe "managing to outcomes"—an overarching ethic of rigorously pursuing meaningful, measurable good for those we serve—can and must become a viral concept in the social sector.

After years of incremental gains, our sector is more than ready for a quantum leap. It's time to dramatically increase our collective impact precisely when we're needed the most.

I qualified for AARP membership a long time ago, so I don't have forever to wait. And, much more important, neither do the hundreds of millions of people around the globe who need us to take on the difficult, even the impossible, and do it with a commitment to be as effective as we possibly can be.

Take-Homes in Tweets

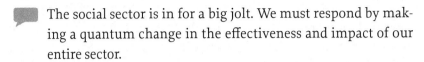 The social sector is in for a big jolt. We must respond by making a quantum change in the effectiveness and impact of our entire sector.

We must help nonprofits and funders alike understand the "value proposition" for managing to outcomes—through data and stories.

We could start a prestigious award, perhaps linked to the Drucker legacy, to build awareness of the importance of managing to outcomes.

We could establish a voluntary program of management certification, based on the successful ISO 9001 quality standards.

We could encourage various kinds of performance-based funding that would explicitly link payments to the achievement of outcomes.

We could support the development of common frameworks within social-sector fields to create efficiencies and greater collective impact.

We don't need to wait for the full force of the fiscal storm to hit before we open our eyes to the truth of what's on the way.

The time to dramatically increase our collective impact is now, when we're needed the most.

Ideas Into Action
A Framework to Get You Started

To bring home and make actionable the key points in this monograph, I offer below a framework that you can use to evolve to the practice of managing to outcomes. This framework is far from perfect, as VPP's investment partners made clear during a wonderfully open and candid discussion we hosted. But it reflects many years of implementing management systems in the private sector and more than a decade of experience in the nonprofit sector to understand what's working, assess performance, and focus on outcomes. It's also informed by a wealth of views from people smarter than I, who have been kind enough to share their thinking over the years and who provided wonderful feedback in response to early versions of this monograph.

As you will see, my starting premise is that it takes a bold spark to ignite outcomes and performance thinking. This spark should emanate from the board as well as the organization's leader, because it is the board's responsibility to ensure that the organization is clear on what change it is focused on creating and also to ensure that the organization is actually delivering on this core purpose.

But, of course, reality is rarely neat and orderly. It may be that a visionary executive or manager—either one who is new to the organization or one who has been with the organization for years—steps forward against all the odds and naysayers and takes responsibility for driving toward a greater outcomes focus.

Framework for Managing to Outcomes

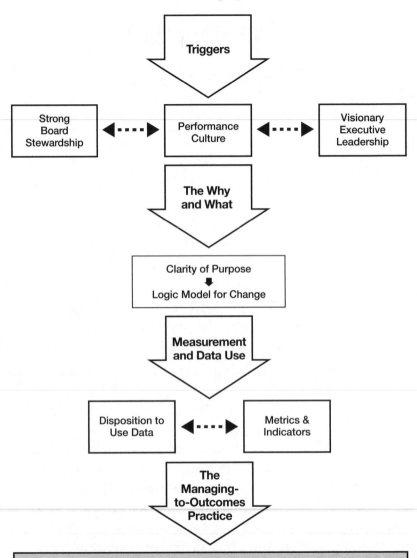

Let me say this as clearly as I can to nonprofits and funders alike: The challenge of managing to outcomes has little to do with systems, processes, or technology. The real challenge is that organizations cannot hope to manage to outcomes unless they have in place an engaged board; leadership with conviction; clarity of purpose; and a supportive performance culture.

Questions to Guide You

These questions are applicable to most, but not all, nonprofits. They are probably most relevant for nonprofits with annual budgets of $2 million or more (not that budget is the only pertinent factor). Although smaller nonprofits cannot be expected to take this on fully, I don't want to hand out too many exemptions or "indulgences." Even small nonprofits should be expected to understand, with at least some level of rigor, what outcomes they would like to achieve, what produces positive results for those they serve, and how they might begin to assess outcomes as they grow larger. And boards should demand this conversation.

TRIGGERS

Strong Board Stewardship

- Does your board know what the organization does to produce positive results, how the organization actually delivers its services, and how it is run?

- Does your board see governance and stewardship as leadership, where board members and executives work together to ensure the success of the organization, or is the board primarily focused on fundraising?

- Does your board accept responsibility for overseeing the organization's quality and ensure that what you do benefits those you serve in material, measurable, and sustainable ways?

My Core Assumptions

The board of directors must take every step necessary to ensure that the organization has clarity of purpose, the right leadership in place, and a performance culture. It must also have a deep understanding of those the organization serves and the outcomes it aims to achieve. It must have the wherewithal to codify and assess what it does, course-correct, and improve. When it comes to managing to outcomes, the buck stops with the executive director. But when it comes to ensuring that the executive director manages to the right outcomes, the buck ultimately stops with the board.

Visionary Executive Leadership

○ Do you have a strong desire and commitment to drive higher performance by managing to outcomes? Are there others on your senior leadership team who share this commitment?

○ Are the individuals who share a commitment to managing to outcomes the type who "get things done" and have the stature within the organization to influence others?

My Core Assumptions

Evolving your organization to manage to outcomes requires, for most non-profits, a fundamental change in mindset and behavior. This bold change doesn't come from an endless series of planning sessions, outsourcing the task to consultants, or delegating it "to be implemented." It is driven by visionary leaders who are willing and able to disrupt the old way of working and who often show the same obsessive tendencies you see in successful private-sector entrepreneurs. These leaders win over "early adopters" and understand how to introduce change in manageable doses. Ideally, as the lead executive, you are the person who provides this life force.

Performance Culture

- Are you confident that the right people are in the right positions? If not, do you have a plan and the conviction to make necessary changes?

- Has everyone—staff, managers, executive team, and board—fully bought into the reality that, when all is said and done, nothing matters if your organization's beneficiaries have not gained materially, measurably, and sustainably from your products or services?

- Do all members of your organization know in reasonably clear terms what you expect of them?

- Do you take time to work with staff, alone and in teams, to solicit and amplify their best thinking, provide constructive feedback, and candidly but respectfully critique their weaknesses?

My Core Assumptions

Making the commitment to be an outcomes-focused organization is a quantum step, and leadership has to want to do it. You'll need people on your staff who will embrace the learning process and make this transformation happen. Measurement and systems take honed skills to be done right—this is not an opinion, but a demonstrated fact—so you'll need to invest in developing your staff.

Organizations that develop the internal capacity to engage and educate management and staff on the disciplined use of information get great returns and continue to improve over time. Those that don't develop this capacity wind up with an ineffective operation and, eventually, an atrophied system. A performance culture makes the difference.

THE WHY AND WHAT

Clarity of Purpose

○ What is your organization's purpose—that is, what are you in business to do?

○ Can you state clearly whom you are in business to serve? To what degree do you serve only the group or set of groups you intended, and to what degree do you serve others?

○ Is your mission so clear and grounded that executives, managers, and front-line staff members know it; apply it as the litmus test for all decisions and actions; and use it to motivate themselves?

○ What are the guiding principles and/or core beliefs that underpin your organization's very existence, and are they instilled and demonstrated throughout your organization?

○ Does your board keep you focused on your mission, guiding principles, and intended beneficiaries?

○ Do you make time to revisit and refine your purpose and strategies, with input from those you serve, on a regular basis?

My Core Assumptions

Having been both villain and victim when it comes to clarity of purpose, I cannot stress enough the importance of being clear and focused on what you do and expect. Be explicitly clear on purpose, guiding principles, and whom you serve. As my good friend Marc Morgenstern so astutely said, "An expectation unarticulated is a disappointment guaranteed." In this case, an intended outcome not articulated and assessed is a disappointment guaranteed!

Logic Model for Change

- ○ Can you clearly define and describe the range of programs and services you provide?

- ○ Can you state clearly the outcomes you are trying to achieve for your intended beneficiaries through each program and service your organization offers?

- ○ Can you define, with reasonable specificity, what each of your programs and services actually does that leads to these outcomes?

- ○ Can you demonstrate that your programs and services are informed by insights from those you serve as well as relevant research and/or the proven practices of others in the field?

My Core Assumptions

An excerpt from "Daniel and the Rhinoceros," which David Hunter wrote when he was director of assessment at the Edna McConnell Clark Foundation, captures my assumptions much better than I can: "The [Edna McConnell Clark] Foundation has learned that grantees benefit from consultations provided in the area of evaluation, in which they are assisted in specifying the group(s) they seek to serve, clarifying outcome objectives for programs' participants, describing program elements through which they intend to help participants achieve targeted outcomes, and identifying the human, material, organizational, and fiscal resources needed to deliver systems as intended.... This amounts to developing a theory of change—a formal rendering of the approach adopted by the organization to change something about the world ... and becomes the guide whereby the organization structures its daily activities to achieve its strategic goals and objectives. It also provides the framework within which each organization can examine what works and what does not work within its own programming and manage performance for continuous improvement."

MEASUREMENT AND DATA USE

Disposition to Use Data

○ Does your organization systematically collect and use information, however basic, to guide your programmatic and operational decisions and execution? In other words, is there a base upon which to build?

○ Can you show tangible examples of how you use information in the daily course of operation? For example, do you have a well-defined budget with regular expense-to-budget reporting? Do you engage in regular collection and reporting of basic operational data (e.g., a school might track the number of applications, enrollment, student turnover, faculty turnover and churn within the year)?

○ Do people at each level buy in to the importance and utility of information as a fundamental benefit and responsibility of their work?

My Core Assumptions

The aphorism "You can lead a horse to water, but you can't make it drink" is especially applicable to measurement, use of data, and managing to outcomes. All the flashy systems, aesthetics, and favorable circumstances won't make someone do something he or she doesn't want to do. At the outset, don't make the mistake of mandating or imposing. Instead, seek out and work with those who have a demonstrated predisposition to use information to do what they do better—or who at least are not set against it. Past behaviors are reasonable predictors of staff members' affinity for a performance-management approach. Orchestrate it so that front-line staff have early victories when working with data, and then highlight these victories so that the whole staff sees how data can help them do their jobs better. As the value becomes clearer, others will come on board.

Metrics and Indicators

- Can you identify the two or three most important pieces of information for managing to your outcomes?

- Can you define the few leading indicators that help you determine if you are doing the right things to eventually achieve the outcomes you intend for those you serve?

- Are the people at various levels of your organization intimately involved in identifying the information that they need to do their jobs and that you need to guide your efforts?

My Core Assumptions

Think of each outcome as what you have to manage toward. Ask what you need to know that will tell you when the outcome has been achieved and what leading indicators inform you that you are on track to get there. Most strong organizations track more than two or three measures, but they prioritize the top two or three to stay focused on what really matters. PLEASE don't make the cardinal sin of "information design"—basing the definition of metrics on what you know is available rather than on what you need!

Be meticulous and absolutely demanding in scrutinizing each metric so you don't drown in data. Ask why you have selected each one. Could there be better ones? Easier ones that would serve as well?

Invest heavily in defining your first set of metrics while also recognizing that this will be a continuous learning process and that the metrics and your ability to use them will evolve over time.

THE MANAGING-TO-OUTCOMES PRACTICE

Performance-Management Mindset and System

○ Is responsibility for establishing a performance-management mindset, process, and system vested in a senior member of the leadership team who has a title such as Chief/Head of Mission Effectiveness?

○ Have you encapsulated and codified the metrics and indicators into an organized system that regularly collects, assimilates, stores, analyzes, and reports on the information and is accessible for inquiry?

○ Is there a professional who truly understands how to read data—that is, who understands what goes with what, who can see patterns in numbers, who can interpret trends for others?

○ Does the organization understand the importance in investing in such people?

○ Is the board "on board" with ensuring sufficient funds are in place to support such investment?

○ As demanding as this may sound, is the system designed to be simple, intuitive, visually appealing, and fast?

○ Are staff, managers, executives, and the board sufficiently trained in how the performance-management system works so they can monitor and manage their own performance and the performance of staff under their scope of responsibility?

○ Do you expect—even demand—that staff and managers apply relevant information (planning, operational, demographics, etc.) to drive decision making and execution?

○ Is there a high adoption rate by leadership and staff in using the system itself and information that comes from it?

○ Are you willing to share your organization's performance with your board? With your funders? With those you serve?

○ Do you have processes in place to explore and improve your system over time?

My Core Assumptions

The definition of "system" is "a set of interacting or interdependent entities forming an integrated whole." The inanimate entities of a performance-management system are the raw data, collection processes, information architecture, data store, reports, and user interface. But the leadership and staff bring life to the data and processes through keen judgment and decision making; curiosity and desire for continuous improvement; and the technical know-how to ensure system integrity and accuracy.

No performance-management system is perfect, so the strongest organizations encourage continuous refinement of their systems to make them simpler, more intuitive, more visually appealing, and more beneficial.

Compendium of Top Readings for Mission Effectiveness

━━━

This section provides a directory of articles, reports, books, and tools that amplify key themes of this monograph and will help you take the leap toward greater mission effectiveness. The materials are aligned to the Managing to Outcomes framework we shared on p. 64.

We're proud of this compendium, but we don't claim that it is definitive; the list surely reflects sins of omission and commission on our part. Please help us improve it by visiting the living version at leapofreason.org/compendium.

This compendium benefited from the sage advice of Laura Callanan and director emeritus Les Silverman, McKinsey & Company; David Carrier and David Murphey, Child Trends; Michael Connolly, VMware; Matt Forti and Nan Stone, The Bridgespan Group; A. Marc Harrison, James Merlino, and Sarah Sinclair, Cleveland Clinic Foundation; David E. K. Hunter, Hunter Consulting; Fred Miller, The Chatham Group; Amy Main Morgenstern, Main Stream Enterprises; Nancy Osgood, The Osgood Group; and Victoria Vrana, Venture Philanthropy Partners.

To compile this first version of the compendium, we followed a process we have used with great success over the years:

- **Determine the experts.** We focused on identifying the top experts for each topic rather than attempting to do a layperson's deep dive. Part of our ongoing learning process is to cultivate relationships with smart people who have knowledge and skills that far surpass our own.

- **Ask for help.** As long as you don't abuse relationships by making too many requests, people generally like to be asked for their input. Our first email went to more than twenty people, our roster of "rock stars" on these particular topics. The response rate was about 75 percent.

- **Give examples.** To help the outside experts understand what we were looking for, our internal team created a starter set of citations in each category. This helped ensure that we received relevant feedback.

- **Scrub, rinse, and repeat.** We're big believers in the iterative process. Over a three-month span, we went back to these highly respected colleagues twice more after our initial ask to further refine the list of resources. Each time the compendium got stronger.

We have organized the compendium into thirteen categories:

- Overarching Themes

- Strong Board Stewardship

- Performance Culture

- Visionary Executive Leadership

- Clarity of Purpose

- Logic Model for Change

- Disposition to Use Data

- Metrics and Indicators

- Performance-Management Mindset and Systems

- Tools for Managing to Outcomes

- Building the Case for Managing to Outcomes

- Managing-to-Outcomes Examples/Case Studies

- Other Relevant Topics

Each section provides our working definition of the category; Zagat-like introductory comments drawn from our experts' assessments; and citations with links to the materials (in short form, to make them easier to type into a browser for those viewing this monograph in hard copy). Links may provide direct access to the resource, a venue for purchasing it, or an interview or article that mentions the resource and provides additional context.

Overarching Themes
Resources that address how to drive change, improve effectiveness, and achieve greatness

We've listed six valuable resources in this category. The first three are, in the estimation of our experts, "must reads." In the two *Good to Great* studies, Jim Collins explains that leaders of great organizations must confront brutal facts. Nonprofits without a focus on outcomes may find it impossible to know or understand the importance of their own key brutal facts. In *Competing on Analytics*, Tom Davenport and Jeanne Harris provide high-profile examples that show how companies are using tools to accelerate innovation, optimize their effectiveness, and identify the true drivers behind their missions—work that we believe has transfer value to the social sector.

- Collins, James C. ***Good to Great and the Social Sectors: Why Business Thinking Is Not the Answer: A Monograph to Accompany Good to Great.*** Boulder, CO: J. Collins, 2005 | leapofreason.org/CollinsSocialSector

- Collins, James C. ***Good to Great: Why Some Companies Make the Leap—And Others Don't.*** New York: Harperbusiness, 2001 | leapofreason.org/CollinsGoodtoGreat

- Davenport, Thomas H., and Jeanne G. Harris. ***Competing on Analytics: The New Science of Winning.*** Boston: Harvard Business School Press, 2007 | leapofreason.org/Davenport

- Green, Alison, and Jerry Hauser. ***Managing to Change the World: The Nonprofit Leader's Guide to Getting Results.*** Washington, DC: Management Center, 2009 | leapofreason.org/Green

- Kotter, J. P. **"Leading Change: Why Transformation Efforts Fail."** *Harvard Business Review*, March-April 1995 | leapofreason.org/Kotter

- Sheehan, Robert M. ***Mission Impact: Breakthrough Strategies for Nonprofits.*** Hoboken, NJ: Wiley, 2010 | leapofreason.org/Sheehan

Strong Board Stewardship
Resources that discuss the importance of strong boards, what defines them, and how they function, especially with respect to mission effectiveness and assessment

Our experts gave "The New Work of the Nonprofit Board," "Mission-Driven Governance," and "More Effective Boards: A Detailed Guide" the highest rankings. As the authors of "More Effective Boards" note, "Beyond *what* to do, *how* the board does its work is equally important." All of the resources in this category can help spark good conversations in your organization.

○ Fisman, Raymond, Rakesh Khurana, and Edward Martenson. **"Mission-Driven Governance."** *Stanford Social Innovation Review*, Summer 2009 | leapofreason.org/Fisman (subscribers only)

○ Jansen, Paul, and Andrea Kilpatrick. **"The Dynamic Nonprofit Board."** *McKinsey Quarterly*, May 2004 | leapofreason.org/Jansen

○ **"More Effective Boards: A Detailed Guide."** In *Bridgestar: Nonprofit Jobs, Careers, and Boards of Directors*. Boston: Bridgespan Group, 2009 | leapofreason.org/Bridgespan

○ *The Source: Twelve Principles of Governance That Power Exceptional Boards.* Washington, DC: BoardSource, 2005 | leapofreason.org/BoardSource

○ Taylor, Barbara E., Richard Chait, and Thomas Holland. **"The New Work of the Nonprofit Board."** *Harvard Business Review*, September 1996 | leapofreason.org/TaylorChait

Performance Culture
Resources that discuss the importance of organizational culture and its vital role for organizations seeking to manage to outcomes

McKinsey & Company defines performance culture as "the connective tissue that binds together the organization, including shared values and practices, behavior norms, and most important, the organization's orientation towards performance." As many of the resources below illustrate, a performance culture must be developed from within. In *SuperCorp*, Rosabeth Moss Kanter illustrates how companies use their strong cultures to adapt and innovate; these tenets are equally applicable to nonprofit organizations. Jeffrey Sonnenfeld's article in the *Harvard Business Review* emphasizes the importance of building a highly accountable culture within the board.

- Connors, Roger, and Tom Smith. ***Change the Culture, Change the Game: The Breakthrough Strategy for Energizing Your Organization and Creating Accountability for Results.*** New York: Portfolio Penguin, 2011 | leapofreason.org/Connors

- Friedman, Mark. ***Trying Hard Is Not Good Enough.*** Bloomington, IN: Trafford Publishing, 2005 | leapofreason.org/Friedman

- Hogan, Cornelius, and David Murphey. ***Outcomes: Reframing Responsibility for Well-Being: A Report to the Annie E. Casey Foundation.*** Baltimore: Annie E. Casey Foundation, 2002 | leapofreason.org/Hogan

- Kanter, Rosabeth Moss. ***SuperCorp: How Vanguard Companies Create Innovation, Profits, Growth, and Social Good.*** New York: Crown Business, 2009 | leapofreason.org/Kanter

- Schorr, Lisbeth B. ***Common Purpose: Strengthening Families and Neighborhoods to Rebuild America.*** New York: Anchor Books, Doubleday, 1997 | leapofreason.org/Schorr

- Sonnenfeld, Jeffrey. **"What Makes Great Boards Great."** *Harvard Business Review*, September 2002 | leapofreason.org/Sonnenfeld

- **"Transforming Giants."** *Harvard Business School Summit*, October 2008 | leapofreason.org/HBSSummit

Visionary Executive Leadership

Resources that provide insights into the leadership qualities that are most valuable for creating organizational change and performance

All three citations below received "must-read" ratings in our outreach. *HBR*'s *10 Must Reads on Leadership* offers insights from a compelling lineup of leadership gurus; it's a seminar in a single volume.

○ Goleman, Daniel, Peter F. Drucker, John P. Kotter, Ronald A. Heifetz, Donald L. Laurie, Robert Goffee, Gareth Jones, Warren G. Bennis, Robert J. Thomas, Jim Collins, David Rooke, William R. Torbert, William W. George, Peter Sims, Andrew N. McLean, Diana Mayer, Deborah Ancona, Thomas W. Malone, Wanda J. Orlikowski, and Peter M. Senge. ***HBR's 10 Must Reads on Leadership.*** Boston: Harvard Business School Publishing, 2010 | leapofreason.org/Goleman

○ Heifetz, Ronald, and Marty Linksy. **"A Survival Guide for Leaders."** *Harvard Business Review*, June 2002 | leapofreason.org/Heifetz

○ Taylor, William. **"Leader of the Future."** *Fast Company*, May 1999 | leapofreason.org/TaylorLeader

Clarity of Purpose

Resources that focus on why it's important to have a clear direction and how to develop such clarity

Any resource by Peter Drucker will get high rankings in most circles. Our colleagues at McKinsey and Bridgespan provide great insights as well. They underscore the value of developing a clarity of focus that reflects the organization's opportunities, core competencies, and commitment.

○ Colby, Susan, Nan Stone, and Paul Carttar. **"Zeroing In on Impact."** *Stanford Social Innovation Review*, Fall 2004 | leapofreason.org/Colby

○ Drucker, Peter. ***Managing the Nonprofit Organization: Principles and Practice.*** New York: HarperCollins, 1990 | leapofreason.org/DruckerManaging

○ Kilpatrick, Andrea, and Les Silverman. **"The Power of Vision."** *Strategy & Leadership*, Spring 2005 | leapofreason.org/Kilpatrick

Logic Model for Change

Resources that define the concept of a logic model for change or a theory of change—that is, how programs and services come together to achieve the organization's intended outcomes

We believe that all the resources we've listed below deserve "must-read" status. These individuals and organizations are true authorities and good explainers.

- Brest, Paul. **"The Power of Theories of Change."** *Stanford Social Innovation Review*, Spring 2010 | leapofreason.org/BrestTheoriesofChange

- Child Trends. **"Child Trends Evaluation Resources."** | leapofreason.org/ChildTrendsEvaluation

- Child Trends. **"LINKS (Lifecourse Interventions to Nurture Kids Successfully)."** | leapofreason.org/ChildTrendsLINKS

- Hunter, David E. K. **"Using a Theory of Change Approach to Build Organizational Strength, Capacity and Sustainability with Not-for-Profit Organizations in the Human Services Sector."** *Evaluation and Program Planning*, May 2006 | leapofreason.org/HunterTheoryofChange

- W. K. Kellogg Foundation. *Logic Model Development Guide.* Battle Creek, MI: W. K. Kellogg Foundation, 2004. | leapofreason.org/Kellogg

- **"Mapping Change: Using a Theory of Change to Guide Planning and Evaluation."** GrantCraft, a project of the Foundation Center and the European Foundation Centre | leapofreason.org/GrantCraft

Disposition to Use Data

Resources that identify traits and behaviors that reveal whether or not leaders are comfortable using data to guide key organizational decisions

We had a difficult time coming up with suggestions for this section; perhaps it's one of those gray areas requiring more art than science. Fortunately, David Hunter provided one article to get you started, and we hope that readers will be able to help flesh out this section in the coming months.

- Hunter, David E. K. **"Daniel and the Rhinoceros."** *Evaluation and Program Planning*, May 2006 | leapofreason.org/HunterRhinoceros

Metrics and Indicators

Resources that put flesh on the terms "metrics," "indicators," "outcomes," and other key concepts that underlie effective measurement

One colleague described *Finding Out What Matters for Youth* as "a model that uses data to begin to unpack the 'black box' between activities and outcomes, including questions of 'dosage.'" One other top read in this category is "Positive Indicators of Child Well-Being," which is viewed as one of the definitive sources of metrics and indicators in the field of child development.

○ Gambone, Michelle, Adena Klem, and James Connell. ***Finding Out What Matters for Youth: Testing Key Links in a Community Action Framework for Youth Development.*** Hamilton, NJ: Youth Development Strategies, 2002 | leapofreason.org/Gambone

○ Lippman, Laura, Kristin Anderson Moore, and Hugh McIntosh. **"Positive Indicators of Child Well-Being: A Conceptual Framework, Measures and Methodological Issues."** *Innocenti Working Paper*, October 2009 | leapofreason.org/Lippman

○ National Institute on Drug Abuse. **"Promise Neighborhoods Research Consortium: What Works."** Promise Neighborhoods Research Consortium | leapofreason.org/NIDA

○ Sawhill, John, and David Williamson. **"Measuring What Matters in Nonprofits."** *McKinsey Quarterly*, May 2001 | leapofreason.org/Sawhill

○ Terzian, Mary, Kristin Anderson Moore, Lisa Williams-Taylor, and Hoan Nguyen. **"Online Resources for Identifying Evidence-Based, Out-of-School Time Programs: A User's Guide."** Child Trends Research Briefs | leapofreason.org/Terzian

○ Urban Institute, Child Trends, and Social Solutions. **"Outcomes and Effective Practices Portal."** Forthcoming Winter 2011 | leapofreason.org/OEPP

○ Wheatley, Margaret, and Myron Kellner-Rogers. **"What Do We Measure and Why? Questions about the Uses of Measurement."** *Journal for Strategic Performance Measurement*, June 1999 | leapofreason.org/Wheatley

Performance-Management Mindset and Systems
Resources that discuss what's needed to mentally prepare for, establish, and use performance-management systems

Howard Dresner's work was recommended by the Cleveland Clinic Foundation group as a very good source. While it is written as a guide for private-sector organizations, there is good transfer value for nonprofits. In "Performance Management and Evaluation: What's the Difference?" Child Trends scholars Karen Walker and Kristin Moore discuss the similarities and the differences between performance management and evaluation, the purposes of collecting information, the timing of data collection, the people primarily responsible for the investigation, and how benchmarks are derived and used. It's a succinct and helpful explanation of concepts often misunderstood.

- ○ Dresner, Howard. *The Performance Management Revolution: Business Results Through Insight and Action.* Hoboken, NJ: Wiley, 2008 | leapofreason.org/DresnerRevolution

- ○ Hatry, Harry P. *Performance Measurement: Getting Results, Second Edition.* Washington, DC: Urban Institute Press, 2006 | leapofreason.org/Hatry

- ○ Howson, Cindi. *Successful Business Intelligence: Secrets to Making BI a Killer App.* New York: McGraw-Hill, 2008 | leapofreason.org/Howson

- ○ ICMA (International City/County Management Association). **"ICMA Performance Measurement KnowledgeNetwork."** | leapofreason.org/ICMA

- ○ Liner, Blaine, Harry P. Hatry, Elisa Vinson, Ryan Allen, Pat Dusenbury, Scott Bryant, and Ron Snell. *Making Results-Based State Government Work.* Washington, DC: Urban Institute, 2001 | leapofreason.org/Liner

- ○ Miles, Marty, Sheila Maguire, Stacy Woodruff-Bolte, and Carol Clymer. *Putting Data to Work: Interim Recommendations from the Benchmarking Project.* Philadelphia: Public/Private Ventures, 2010 | leapofreason.org/Miles

- ○ Penna, Robert M. *The Nonprofit Outcomes Toolbox: A Complete Guide to Program Effectiveness, Performance Measurement, and Results.* Hoboken, NJ: Wiley, 2011 | leapofreason.org/Penna

○ Taylor, James, and Neil Raden. *Smart (Enough) Systems: How to Deliver Competitive Advantage by Automating Hidden Decisions.* Harlow, England: Prentice Hall, 2007 | leapofreason.org/TaylorRaden

○ United Way of America. *Measuring Program Outcomes: A Practical Approach.* Alexandria, VA: United Way of America, 1996 | leapofreason.org/UnitedWay

○ Walker, Karen E., and Kristin Anderson Moore. **"Performance Management and Evaluation: What's the Difference?"** Child Trends, January 2011 | leapofreason.org/Walker

○ Winkler, Mary K., Brett Theodos, and Michel Gross. *Evaluation Matters: Lessons from Youth-Serving Organizations.* Washington, DC: Urban Institute, 2009 | leapofreason.org/Winkler

○ Wolk, Andrew, Anand Dholakia, and Kelley Kreitz. *Building a Performance Measurement System: Using Data to Accelerate Social Impact.* Cambridge, MA: Root Cause, 2009 | leapofreason.org/Wolk

Tools for Managing to Outcomes
Resources that present methods, systems, and models to prepare for and ingrain managing to outcomes

We believe that tools, systems, and methods come into play as a result of your strategic direction rather than in place of it, but we recognize that leaders need frameworks to adapt. Here are two tools that may assist your efforts. The Center for Effective Philanthropy helps funders gauge their performance relative to peer foundations. The Organizational Capacity Assessment Tool developed by McKinsey & Company for VPP has been cited in more than twenty books and college courses, and more than seventy organizations have requested permission to modify or replicate the tool, post it on their websites, or distribute it to their own grantees.

○ **"Center for Effective Philanthropy Assessment Tools."** Center for Effective Philanthropy | leapofreason.org/CEPTools

○ **"Organizational Capacity Assessment Tool (OCAT)."** *Effective Capacity Building in Nonprofits.* Washington, DC: Venture Philanthropy Partners, prepared by McKinsey & Company, 2001 | leapofreason.org/OCAT

Building the Case for Managing to Outcomes
Resources that present a compelling case for managing to outcomes, which can be very helpful for sparking conversations within boards and leadership teams

Organizations need well-reasoned arguments from credible sources to persuade stakeholders that managing to outcomes can lead to greater mission effectiveness. All of the resources below can help.

- Bradach, Jeffrey, Thomas Tierney, and Nan Stone. **"Delivering on the Promise of Nonprofits."** *Harvard Business Review*, December 2008 | leapofreason.org/Bradach

- Drucker, Peter F. **"What Is the Bottom Line When There Is No 'Bottom Line'?"** In *Managing the Non-Profit Organization: Practices and Principles: Including Interviews with Frances Hesselbein [et al.].* New York: HarperCollins, 1990. 107—112 | leapofreason.org/DruckerBottomLine

- Neuhoff, Alex, and Bob Searle. **"More Bang for the Buck."** *Stanford Social Innovation Review*, Spring 2008 | leapofreason.org/Neuhoff

- Urban Institute and Center for What Works. **"Outcome Indicators Project."** | leapofreason.org/UrbanInstitute

Managing-to-Outcomes Examples/Case Studies
Resources that provide tangible models of managing to outcomes

Seeing the results that other organizations have achieved can be useful as you begin your efforts around managing to outcomes. Here are a few snapshots of managing-to-outcomes initiatives.

- Abelson, Reed. **"Managing Outcomes Helps a Children's Hospital Climb in Renown."** *New York Times*, September 15, 2007 | leapofreason.org/Abelson

- Heath, Chip, and Dan Heath. *Switch: How to Change Things When Change Is Hard.* New York: Broadway Books, 2010 | leapofreason.org/Heath

- Howard, Don, and Susan Colby. *Great Valley Center: A Case Study in Measuring for Mission.* Boston: Bridgespan, 2003 | leapofreason.org/Howard

Other Relevant Topics
Resources that provide context, additional insights, and considerations that may be of help to those transitioning to managing to outcomes

In the view of our experts, these resources below all provide great value and are relevant to managing to outcomes. We've grouped them here because they didn't fit neatly into any of our other categories.

- Brest, Paul, Hal Harvey, and Kelvin Low. **"Calculated Impact."** *Stanford Social Innovation Review*, Winter 2009 | leapofreason.org/BrestHarvey (subscribers only)

- Council of State Governments. **"States Perform."** | leapofreason.org/CouncilStateGovernments

- Dresner, Howard. *Profiles in Performance: Business Intelligence Journeys and the Roadmap for Change.* Hoboken, NJ: John Wiley & Sons, 2010 | leapofreason.org/DresnerProfiles

- Gawande, Atul. *The Checklist Manifesto: How to Get Things Right.* New York: Metropolitan Books, 2010 | leapofreason.org/Gawande

- Kania, John, and Mark Kramer. **"Collective Impact."** *Stanford Social Innovation Review*, Winter 2011 | leapofreason.org/Kania

- *Keystone Guides for Impact Planning, Learning, and Assessment.* London: Keystone Accountability for Social Change, 2009 | leapofreason.org/Keystone

- Kramer, Mark, Marcie Parkhurst, and Lalitha Vaidyanathan. *Breakthroughs in Shared Measurement and Social Impact.* Boston: FSG Social Impact Advisors, 2009 | leapofreason.org/Kramer

- Miller, Clara. **"The Four Horsemen of the Nonprofit Financial Apocalypse."** *Nonprofit Quarterly*, March 2010 | leapofreason.org/Miller

- *New Approaches to Evaluating Community Initiatives.* Washington, DC: Aspen Institute, 1995 | leapofreason.org/AspenInstitute

- *Priorities for a New Decade: Making (More) Social Programs Work (Better).* Philadelphia: Public/Private Ventures, 2011 | leapofreason.org/PPV

○ Scearce, Diane, and Katherine Fulton. **"High Ambitions and Scarce Resources in Public Interest Organizations."** *Development*, August 2004 | leapofreason.org/Scearce

○ Silverstein, Laura, and Erin Maher. **"Evaluation Blues: How Accountability Requirements Hurt Small, Innovative Programs the Most."** *Stanford Social Innovation Review*, Winter 2008 | leapofreason.org/Silverstein

○ Stid, Daniel, and Jeffrey Bradach. **"Strongly Led, Under-Managed: How Can Visionary Nonprofits Make the Critical Transition to Stronger Management?"** *Bridgespan Group*, August 2008 | leapofreason.org/Stid

○ Tierney, Thomas J., and Joel L. Fleishman. *Give Smart: Philanthropy That Gets Results.* New York: PublicAffairs, March 2011 | leapofreason.org/TierneyFleishman

○ **University HealthSystem Consortium** | leapofreason.org/UHC

Essays by Experts and Practitioners
Who Are "Walking the Talk"

First, Do No Harm ... Then Do More Good

by Isaac Castillo

Most nonprofits view collecting information on outcomes for their clients as a daunting task, a waste of resources, or both. However, the process of data collection and outcomes measurement is a critical activity for any nonprofit that seeks to improve the quality of services it provides. Without knowing what they do well and what needs to be improved, nonprofits can end up providing the same services for years without ever really knowing if they could be doing something different that would lead to greater benefits for the population they are serving.

For a nonprofit to provide the best services possible to its clients, it must measure its outcomes. This is easier said than done; frequently the entire culture of the organization must change to become more accepting of the regular collection of outcomes. Fortunately, there are steps that a nonprofit can take to make this culture change more feasible and more lasting.

Changing the Conversation

The first (and perhaps most critical) step in creating a culture of outcomes measurement is getting everyone to understand this simple statement:

A nonprofit should measure outcomes for a single reason: to improve the quality of services for clients.

Far too often, nonprofits think of data collection and evaluation as a chore that has to be done to satisfy funding organizations. This line of reasoning, unfortunately, drives nonprofits to collect only what's required by funders in the short term, rather than information that would allow the organization to determine how to improve services for clients over time.

To avoid this trap, a nonprofit's leadership must change the conversation entirely. Leaders must recognize and then clearly communicate that outcomes measurement is not about simply counting things or gathering information. And it is not about satisfying funders. It is an internal effort aimed at figuring out what works and what doesn't, so that the organization can provide the best possible services to its clients. This approach usually resonates with nonprofit staff, nearly all of whom share a deep commitment to making a difference for those who need assistance.

How Do You Know That Your Organization Is Not Hurting Clients?

Every nonprofit assumes that its programs and services are doing good for its clients. Unfortunately, no organization is perfect. No program is perfect. No individual is perfect. Despite the best of intentions, nonprofits will make mistakes, and those mistakes can cause harm to clients or participants. At the Latin American Youth Center (LAYC), a youth-development agency with multiple locations in the National Capital Region, we learned this lesson the hard way.

In 2007, one of LAYC's parenting programs added some lessons to an existing curriculum. The additional lessons focused on domestic violence issues with the intent of teaching parents that domestic violence is not appropriate in any culture and that there are safe ways to escape domestic violence situations.

When the programming was completed, I analyzed the tests we administered before and after the program. The results were shocking. LAYC's parenting programming, with the additional domestic violence lessons included, actually changed the participants' attitudes toward domestic violence *in the wrong direction*. After finishing our programming, a greater number of participants believed that domestic violence is an appropriate expression of love between partners, that domestic violence is an acceptable part of the Latino culture, and that there is no safe way to leave a violent partner. In a very real sense, our program caused harm to our participants, despite the best of intentions.

Fortunately, because LAYC was collecting information on the participants' attitudes before and after the program, we were able to make important changes to this program before starting with the next group of participants. In the original domestic violence classes we had provided the instruction in a mixed-gender environment. After seeing the negative results, we consulted with domestic violence experts and then split the classes into separate classrooms for men and women so that each could feel more comfortable expressing their feelings. This change, along with others, brought positive, statistically significant changes in attitude in every single cohort.

Making Good Use of the Data We Collect

Once staff members have bought into the idea of outcomes measurement, the next critical step is getting them to actually use the data they are collecting. This means creating reports and data summaries that staff can easily utilize to make decisions. Collecting data is important, but if the data are never used to influence decisions or change programs, then they do not benefit clients.

In LAYC's residential and housing programs, staff members have taken this message to heart. Every six months staff examine nineteen independent-living skill areas (e.g., personal hygiene, money management, housekeeping) and the progress made by residents. For those areas where residents fail to show progress or actually demonstrate regression in skills, residential staff increase the amount of instruction (at the group and individual level) to offer greater reinforcement of lessons and skills. These extra hours are redistributed from instruction on skill areas where residents are showing significant progress.

In this way, staff can change their instructional patterns to match the needs of residents.

By providing staff with information to help them refine and adjust their work, an organization can empower staff to continually improve the quality of services they provide to clients. Data can be a tool to allow staff to serve their clients better, rather than a burden to overcome. This ultimately is how the culture change can be maintained over time.

Using a Theory-of-Change Approach to Helping Nonprofits Manage to Outcomes

by David E. K. Hunter, Ph.D.

———

Along with many others who work in the nonprofit sector, I believe that most claims about nonprofit organizations' ability to deliver results as promised are unsupported by credible evidence. Indeed, I think it is fair to say that the sector suffers generally from a pervasive case of unjustifiable optimism—by which I mean over-claiming non-profits' effectiveness while under-measuring their performance.

Yet, paradoxically, many nonprofits in fact are *over*-measuring. They are, as has been noted by many observers, suffocating under the crushing weight of data—data they collect frantically, often resent-fully, and use mostly to satisfy their diverse funders...but for little else.

So, to ask the famous question, what is to be done? Is there a way for nonprofit organizations to navigate between the serpentine Scylla of unsupportable optimism and the engulfing Charybdis of mind-numbing over-measurement? Yes there is. In a nutshell, the answer is to develop robust theories of change that serve as blueprints for achieving specific results in well-defined domains—that is, to make their strategic visions operational.

Making Theory of Change a Practical Reality

To simplify the matter a bit in this short essay, a theory of change for social service nonprofits consists of a series of "if → then" state-ments that add up to a prescription for the design and management of an organization and the services it delivers in order to help the population(s) it targets achieve key, socially meaningful outcomes.

It's worth emphasizing that any theory of change can be useful only if it is tailored to serve a clear purpose. For example, if the object is to support the design, implementation, and evaluation of a new service program (say preventing drug and alcohol abuse among teenagers), a solid theory of change most likely will focus narrowly on issues of target population, program/service elements, dosage and duration of service utilization, and outcomes. But if the organization is farther along and the purpose is to help it to deliver current programming more broadly and sustainably, then a useful theory of change will need to expand its scope: It will need to address not only program issues, but also organizational and financial matters.

I have developed a four-day approach to helping nonprofits develop theories of change tailored to their specific ambitions and needs. I insist on working with *vertically integrated teams* consisting of representation from the board, executive leadership, mid-level management, and a sampling of front-line staff. In these workshops we review in great detail the organization's mission; goals; objectives; target population; targeted outcomes; key indicators for managing performance and assessing success; organizational capacities; the degree of alignment among its constituent parts (e.g., multiple programs, multiple sites); data gathering and use at all levels of the organization to manage performance; and systematic efforts to learn from performance and understand whether the organization's efforts are achieving outcomes as intended. I work to help the group achieve consensus on all these matters, and where this is not possible, to have the executive director commit to a fully transparent process for making an executive decision.

When successful, these workshops have two results: (a) an *output*, consisting of a very detailed blueprint that shows not only each step the organization will be taking to achieve alignment with its mission but also each step it will take to manage at high levels of performance, effectiveness, and efficiency; and (b) an *outcome*, in that the organization moves to a new level of clarity about its mission; high transparency regarding its operations; substantial alignment among its various operational units behind the achievement of its mission, goals, and objectives; a deeper and more realistic understanding of its resource needs; a new view of accountability for results; and a highly focused, streamlined approach to gathering and using performance data to support the achievement of success.

For example:

○ Our Piece of the Pie (Hartford, CT) realized that its legacy program of elderly services and its open-enrollment daycare center bore no relation to its mission to help inner-city, low-income young people successfully transition to adulthood. It decided to limit daycare access to teenage mothers and redesigned elderly services as a social enterprise providing stipends and work-readiness training—both dedicated to helping young people in its case-management program.

○ Juma Ventures (San Francisco, now replicating in San Diego) decided to pull back its early growth efforts in order to deepen its target population to include first- and second-year (low-income) high school students (because starting, as it had, with third-year students could not provide sufficient program dosage and duration to assure the attainment of its educational and work-related outcomes) and implement intensive case-management services.

○ Congreso de Latinos Unidos (Philadelphia) serves individuals and families living mostly in the city's North End and other predominantly Latino neighborhoods. In the theory-of-change workshops, Congreso consolidated some sixty semi-autonomous, contract-driven programs with an aggregate of several hundred outcomes into a core case-management program with three key outcomes (health, education, and employment). The old programs became specialized services; clients develop individualized service plans and "pathways" through the system as their individual needs dictate. In other words, Congreso moved from being "program-centric" to being "client-centric."

○ Summer Search (a national organization headquartered in San Francisco) significantly clarified its target population; revised its ways of talking and working with teens; and abandoned some legacy practices that could not survive rigorous scrutiny.

○ The Center for Employment Opportunities (New York, NY, and now replicating upstate) helps prisoners transition into employment upon their release. As part of developing its theory of change, the organization studied its participants and found that its success with young adults (age 18–24) was much lower than with adults—and as a result built youth development practices into its programming for its younger clients that increased its effectiveness with them. A recent, rigorous evaluation has shown that the organization significantly reduces recidivism.

○ Roca (Chelsea and now also Springfield, MA) scaled back its service capacity for several years to rethink and codify its use of "transformational relationships" and allocate its resources more effectively to help gang- and street-involved young adults leave violence behind and gain sustained employment.

While it is essential that nonprofits develop theories of change, this is just the first step. To become high performing, they must implement (build) what is called for in the blueprint. In general, it takes anywhere from three to six years. In the cases mentioned above, the organizations went on to reconsider board responsibilities; rethink fundraising strategies and goals; redesign organizational structures; deepen management capacities; introduce new HR systems with clear accountability for results; and design and implement performance-management data systems that capture who gets served, the delivery of all elements of programming as codified, monitoring of service quality, appropriate service utilization, and the achievement of outcomes.

Are You Ready for Change?

Is this theory-of-change approach suitable to all nonprofits? No! In my experience there are a few indicators that a nonprofit is ready to undertake this kind of work, all of which must be present for the exercise to yield the kinds of results I have described:

1. **Executive leadership.** The executive director must have arrived at the view that the organization may well not be delivering what it promises, and also must find this situation intolerable (and hence be ready to make very tough decisions). By the way, contrary to the views held by many, I have never seen a board that has driven the commitment to redesign a nonprofit in order to become high-performing and effective.

2. **Board support.** The board must be willing to engage in the process even though it recognizes that in all likelihood more will be required of it as a result—especially with regard to fundraising.

3. **Financial solvency.** An organization must have a sense that it is sustainable before it can participate wholeheartedly in such a workshop. If it is struggling to pay its rent or meet payroll, it is very unlikely that it will have the "space" to take a step back and wrestle with fundamental issues.

4. **Organizational culture.** The organization must have a strong and widely shared sense that it needs data to manage well and work effectively—even if, so far, such efforts have been unfocused, funder-driven, burdensome, and mostly useless in people's daily work.

Conclusion

Bring up performance management with many nonprofit leaders and you've got a good chance of watching their eyes glaze over or widen with fear and loathing. Performance management conjures up the worst dehumanizing practices of the corporate sector and reeks of data gathering run amok.

But this need not be the case. If a nonprofit really knows what it is doing and why—if it has a theory of change that is meaningful (to key stakeholders), plausible (in that it makes sense to stakeholders and key experts), doable (within the resources and capacities of the organization and, perhaps, its strategic partners), assessable (with measurable indicators of progress and success), and monitorable (with well-articulated implementation and performance standards), then designing simple, useful performance metrics really isn't forbiddingly hard, and managing to outcomes can be a reality.

Those who depend on nonprofits in order to overcome structural and individual obstacles and to improve their lives and prospects deserve no less.

Managing to Outcomes: Mission Possible

by Tynesia Boyea Robinson

———

I have implemented performance-management systems in both for-profit and nonprofit settings. As counterintuitive as this sounds, I'm convinced that most nonprofits are just as well suited to manage to outcomes as their for-profit counterparts.

Why? The simple answer is that nonprofits are highly mission-driven.

Most nonprofits attract people who have self-selected based on the mission of the organization. As a result, the nonprofit professionals' passions and interests usually align directly with their organization's reason for existence. Such an alignment gives these professionals intrinsic motivation. (Daniel H. Pink explores this concept beautifully in his book *Drive: The Surprising Truth About What Motivates Us*.)

The assumption underlying the typical performance-management system in the for-profit world is the need for *extrinsic* motivators. If I can reward or reprimand you based on the outcomes, the team will be aligned around the goals we are trying to achieve.

This is not to say that people who work in the private sector don't love their jobs or aren't motivated! It's just that what motivates them about their job is often the what and the how of their role in the company rather than the company's overall mission. A software engineer, for example, might be more motivated by the elegance of the technology he or she is developing than by the company's impact on its customers or in the marketplace.

In my experience, building a performance-management system that taps into intrinsic motivation involves three essential ingredients:

- Creating a feedback culture

- Becoming bilingual

- Relieving the pain.

Creating a Feedback Culture

The nonprofit industry attracts incredibly passionate people who bleed mission. Nonprofit employees are usually underpaid and under-resourced, but many still find time on the weekend to stop by a client's home or walk door to door collecting signatures on a petition to change a policy affecting their constituents.

Performance-management evangelists often say things like "Nonprofits that truly care about their mission will embrace data collection and analysis." This is a huge mistake. In fact, this approach, while harmless in intention, has derailed more performance-management initiatives than I care to think about. Most nonprofit professionals find such statements offensive and may respond defensively, saying something along the lines of "I don't need an expensive IT system to tell me what needs to be fixed" or "These issues are so complex that there's no data that can possibly capture the nuances."

Therefore, before any system is even discussed, the first step is to create a feedback culture.

This does not have to be an extensive exercise. It can start with weekly staff meetings where people share "plus/deltas" (what went well, what should be changed). It is very difficult to tell someone who is working weekends that his or her efforts are not leading to the outcomes that align with the mission. But by building an organizational culture around shared feedback and change, people will be more mentally prepared for what happens when data are at everyone's fingertips. Ideally, feedback should include the perspective of clients, since client feedback underscores the connection to the mission and may diffuse tension.

In order to produce true culture change, the leader must be both vulnerable and committed to change based on staff feedback. Gerald Chertavian, Year Up's founder and CEO, uses town halls with staff across the country not only to gather input on what to do differently but also to publicly acknowledge mistakes he has made. "We owe it to the young adults we serve to be relentless in learning from our mistakes so they can continue to have the opportunities that are commensurate with their talent," he says. By both acknowledging his mistakes and using language that centers on our ultimate goal, Gerald creates an environment where the team wholeheartedly embraces feedback.

Becoming Bilingual

If you put for-profit and nonprofit professionals in a room together, there's often a big cultural divide. For-profit professionals often unintentionally use language that may come across as patronizing and condescending to their nonprofit counterparts. On the other side, nonprofit professionals can display holier-than-thou self-righteousness.

To be successful at performance management, both sides must seek to understand before asking to be understood. As I reflect on my first years as a board member of a nonprofit theater company (soon after I left a Fortune 500 company), I cringe when I think about how I often fell into this trap. My fellow board members and I pushed the theater staff for data on return on investment for set design. We graphed which types of performances were most profitable. And we even began inserting ourselves in program selection. The staff often considered us "corporate outsiders" who did not exhibit heart for the mission.

Instead of getting riled up about statistical significance and trends, we would have been better served by trying to understand what the executives got riled up about. Eventually we learned that what was important to them was the role that the theater's art played in creating dialogue in the community and representing the voice of a systematically underrepresented demographic.

What drives the passion in your nonprofit? Perhaps it's the light in a child's eyes when she grasps a new concept or the beauty of seeing an abandoned landscape converted into a family-friendly park. If you can tap into that passion and then *translate* the wonky world of data into the language of mission, it is far more likely that nonprofit professionals will buy in to the need for performance management. Don't believe me? Which of the following messages would resonate more with you?

Building a performance-management system is critical to enhancing sustainability to ensure that you fulfill your organization's mission.

OR

Please help me understand what it takes to serve your clients well. With your coaching, we can find ways to ensure that we consistently fulfill the mission we're both passionate about.

This may not seem like a breakthrough concept, but it's amazing how many outcomes initiatives fail simply because of language.

Relieving the Pain

Of course, it's easy to say that data and analysis are the panacea for all nonprofit woes. But let's face it: We have many standardized tests and data systems that create additional work with very little change in outcomes. These systems often fail because they stay at the macro level. Imagine the consternation of the nonprofit professional who witnesses the investing of millions of dollars in an IT system to produce a report that says, "Our analysis has shown that schools are failing." The response is usually "You needed millions of dollars for that? I could have told you that for free!"

The real need is to go deeper—to gauge not just whether something is working or not, but to understand *why*. To get more granular, you must first establish credibility with the service providers by making their lives easier, not harder.

If you are working within a feedback culture and speaking in authentic, mission-focused language, it will be easy to spot opportunities for reducing pain for service providers. At most organizations the wish list is a mile long. If you address a few of the big concerns, you'll soon find that the outcomes initiative has transitioned from a "push" to a "pull."

When Year Up set out to implement the Salesforce enterprise data system, for example, COO Sue Meehan engaged our admissions teams from the beginning. Team members were initially skeptical that Salesforce could make their lives easier. With their help, however, Sue built out our Salesforce system not only to make the admissions process smoother and quicker but also to help the admissions teams identify the students who, based on key indicators from previous classes of students, were most likely to benefit from our high-support, high-expectations culture. We've now seen a subtle but hugely significant shift from "Why do we need Salesforce?" to "Why doesn't Salesforce have everything we need?"

Conclusion

Performance management is not easy. It takes a rare (and sometimes at odds) combination of tenacity and sensitivity to pull it off. But when it's done right—when it truly taps into the intrinsic connection to mission that so many nonprofit professionals bring to their jobs day in and day out—then the results can be profound. Passionate people, empowered with data, can do remarkable things to drive performance—and, more important, transform lives.

Performance Management

The Neglected Step in Becoming an Evidence-Based Program

by Kristin Anderson Moore, Ph.D., Karen Walker, Ph.D.,
and David Murphey, Ph.D.

———

The current focus on being "evidence-based" has drawn considerable attention to the value of random-assignment and quasi-experimental evaluations, and that's a good thing. Random-assignment evaluations are the exquisite show horses of the evaluation world, while quasi-experimental evaluations are the trotters. These two kinds of evaluations help funders, practitioners, and policymakers identify whether and for whom programs can make a real and lasting difference. Implementation evaluations—another thoroughbred—focus on whether a program is being implemented well and with fidelity. But the focus on these pretty horses has drawn attention away from the workhorses that help programs manage and improve their performance on an ongoing basis—performance-management systems.

The Process of Becoming an Evidence-Based Program

Figure 1 outlines one common process for becoming an organization that uses data to drive performance and better outcomes.

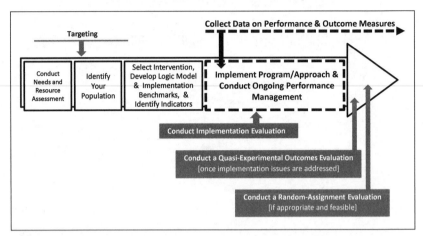

Figure 1: Becoming Performance-Driven

As the figure shows, the initial step involves assessing the risks and needs of a community, along with its available resources, followed by an identification of the groups or places with the highest incidence of these. Following a risk assessment, the focus may shift to identifying programs or intervention strategies that have been evaluated and found to affect the risks or needs of the community. To illustrate, let's say that a risk assessment identifies teen pregnancy as an important issue for a community and, further, that the rate is highest among Latinas. Having identified a program that has been rigorously evaluated and found to reduce the birth rate among Latina teens, the community decides to implement this new program.

Given today's focus on outcome and impact evaluations, a nonprofit may immediately jump ahead and decide to conduct an evaluation of the program as soon as possible. It might be a quasi-experimental or random-assignment evaluation, or perhaps an implementation evaluation. But any of these would be premature. It is first necessary to put a performance-management system in place.

Having such a system enables an organization to monitor program implementation and success over time.

Taking Full Advantage of Performance Management

The term "performance management" covers a broad range of activities. Any program that examines participant characteristics to make sure that the people who enroll are meeting their eligibility requirements is doing performance management. So are programs that ask new participants to complete assessments to determine the services they need, and programs that monitor attendance in activities to make sure that they are engaging their clients.

Most programs do some form of performance management; funding requirements may demand that they serve particular populations or reach certain participation levels. But few programs take full advantage of the power of performance management, which requires the following:

- The capacity to collect and analyze information on an ongoing basis

- Defined benchmarks to assess the progress of participants, the staff, and the program

- Efforts to identify reasons for failing to reach the benchmarks

- The capacity to draw on multiple sources of data to identify the best explanations for a program's challenges

- A willingness to modify programs to address challenges

- The capacity to collect and analyze information to see whether program modifications have addressed the challenges.

Building Your Own "War Room"

Once a program has performance measures, what can you do with them? Most broadly, these become the wall charts prominently displayed in your lobby. Winston Churchill had his "war room," with frequently updated maps and other information about the progress of the Allied and enemy forces. Your program should have the equivalent— the three or four key measures tracking the success of the enterprise. At a more fine-grained level, performance measures can help identify variation—for example, among sites, groups of clients, or program activities—that should prompt further investigation. Why are those folks so much more successful than these folks? What is a particular site doing so well, and how could its success be brought to other sites?

At a still finer level, performance measures can figure in employees' performance evaluations. Performance measures provide a way to act on the genuine desire of staff to "make a difference." The idea here is not to suggest that any one staff person is solely responsible for trends on performance measures, but rather to give employees an opportunity to articulate their own contributions to one or more of the measures, and (ideally) to see their efforts reflected there. But most important, performance management focuses on providing ongoing data on program operations and performance outcomes that can be used to assess and improve program effectiveness.

Data Help WINGS Take Flight

WINGS for Kids is an educational program focused on social-emotional learning. It is designed to teach elementary school children to behave well, make good decisions, and build healthy relationships. To do this, WINGS provides activities five days a week for three hours a day, and children have time to eat, engage in activities of their choice, and do homework or other academic activities in the after-school hours. But it also adds extras: In each day's first thirty minutes, children play games intended to highlight and provide lessons on particular social or emotional skills, such as how to work in teams, have empathy for others, and take responsibility for their actions.

Group leaders (staff members, who are usually college students) are assigned to work with small groups of children. While working with students on the day's academic and free-choice activities, group leaders closely observe the children's behavior to take advantage of "teachable moments" when they have opportunities to intervene, both to redirect negative behavior and to reinforce positive behavior.

As one might imagine, ensuring the quality of a program that employs college students and focuses on improving behavior and social interactions poses challenges. Each year the organization must train new group leaders and ensure that they apply the program's strategies consistently. To address these challenges, program managers have developed a performance-management system that is used diagnostically to ensure that staff are monitoring the students and properly addressing emerging behavioral problems. Group leaders rate children's behaviors on a weekly basis, and supervisors review ratings prior to regular supervision meetings.

Managers also use the system to supervise staff. Group leaders are expected to record a number of "teachable" moments each week, and supervisors read the case notes of those interactions in order to ensure both their quantity and their quality.

Finally, managers use the system to make progress on the program's goals. One of the program's key goals is the improvement of children's behavior during regular school time. Specifically, the program aims for all children to achieve a rating of 85 percent or higher on school behavior, as measured by indicators on the student's report cards such as organizational skills and the ability to work with other students. Several years ago, when managers realized that many children were not reaching the 85 percent benchmark, WINGS added a program component to address in-school behavior. In order to focus on those children's needs and support and encourage communication with teachers, group leaders write individualized student plans and share those with teachers. Although the program has not yet achieved its goal for all students, report cards indicate steady progress.

Conclusion

As critical as good evaluations are, they need to be preceded by and built upon the knowledge provided by a performance-management system. Essentially, this means developing and using your in-house capacity before inviting others in to do expensive random-assignment or implementation evaluations.

What It Takes

Building a Performance-Management System to Support Students and Teachers

by Patricia Brantley

———

At Friendship Public Charter School, we have not shied from controversy in pursuit of better outcomes for our students. Friendship manages four traditional public schools and six public charter schools in Washington, DC, and Baltimore, MD. When Michelle Rhee was chancellor of the DC Public Schools, we partnered with her to turn around DC's most troubled high school, Anacostia Senior High. When Rhee launched one of the country's first performance-based evaluation processes for unionized teachers, Friendship had the distinction of managing these teachers at Anacostia. The media interest in these efforts and in Rhee's pathbreaking partnership with a charter-school operator was unprecedented.

While in general the media have done a good job of explaining why we, the school district, and others are working to use data in much more comprehensive ways (including for evaluating teachers), the media have done very little to illustrate the *how*. In this essay I will try to complete the picture. I'll describe the hard work that has gone into collecting, using, and communicating the data we need in order to assess teachers fairly and support their development in the classroom, and I'll share insights on how we have used these data to engage students and parents more deeply than ever before—a process that has yielded concrete results for our students.

Were We Focusing on the Right Things?

In the 2007–08 school year, Friendship engaged McKinsey & Company to help us design a performance-management system to put mission-critical information in the hands not only of administrators like me but also teachers, parents, and students themselves. A brief note about McKinsey is in order. We feel fortunate to have had the support of such a top-notch firm, and I can't say enough about the smart and caring individuals assigned to our project. But if you don't have the budget to engage a firm like McKinsey, that's fine. There are many consultants with the ability to help you focus, be deliberate, and get results.

The process our consultants organized gave me and other Friendship leaders the opportunity to take a hard, unflinching look at just how focused on performance we really were as leaders and to do the same with each of our staff members. We are all about hard work at Friendship—putting in long hours, constantly working through weekends and holidays. The process with the consultants helped us determine whether all that hard work was smart work. In other words, were we focusing on the right things?

In Friendship's early years, our focus on ensuring the right inputs, such as making sure we had strong teachers and curricula, yielded significant gains for our students. The first Friendship campuses achieved noteworthy performance gains at all grade levels. We widely celebrated our success and began an aggressive expansion strategy. Soon, however, we recognized that performance had begun to flatline. Our schools were still outperforming their peers, but the peaks weren't as high as we had expected. We responded to the flatlining by driving our staff to put in even more time. The exhaustion was becoming apparent—and the results weren't going in the direction we wanted. It was time to call in outside help.

For me, the opportunity to be introspective about our performance meant not just considering the inputs but truly knowing how well those inputs mapped to the outcomes we desired for our students. Further, it gave us a chance to better understand how changing various inputs would yield greater or worse performance—and tie that performance specifically to each person's efforts.

Identifying What Was Worth Measuring

We began the process with McKinsey by identifying the most important "drivers" for delivering on our aspirations for the students who entrust their education to us. At one of our first meetings, we gathered several hundred teachers in our middle school cafeteria to solicit their input on the drivers of success. As any student or parent will tell you, Friendship teachers are warm and welcoming. However, on this particular day, their trepidation was obvious. Teachers had heard that school administrators were going to develop a performance system, but we weren't clear enough with the teachers that they would have an opportunity to guide the work.

A simple, direct question broke the tension in the room: "In your opinion, what's the most important driver?" Soon the conversation was flowing, and we found significant common ground.

After three months of meetings, we arrived at these four drivers:

- Excellent teaching and learning opportunities

- Outstanding leadership teams

- An environment conducive to learning

- Organizational strength and long-term viability.

To make these drivers more than just nice platitudes, we spent the next three months identifying fifteen essential "sub-drivers" and over three hundred key "performance indicators." Figure 1 shows how this worked for a sub-driver of the "Excellent teaching and learning opportunities" driver.

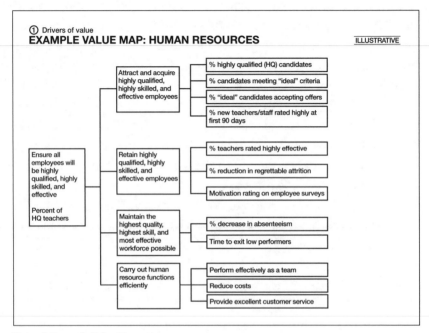

Figure 1: Example Value Map

Arriving at the sub-drivers and indicators was a difficult process and required many hours of internal debate. We assembled a dozen ad hoc teams to help. On each team we carefully placed an "agitator" who would challenge the group by asking, "So what?"

As inclusive as the process was, we didn't always get it right. Just when we were starting to feel good about where we had landed, we discovered we'd missed a critical element: whether the indicators were measurable. As we moved to designing the framework to track sub-drivers and key performance indicators, we found that 15 percent of our indicators were either impossible or impractical to measure.

We made the difficult decision to drop unmeasurable indicators if we could not find a suitable substitute.

Key Lessons From Our Schools

After identifying what mattered—that is, the information worth measuring—we turned to figuring out how to change the culture within our ten schools to collect and then make good use of this information.

At the risk of sounding pedantic, I'd like to offer a few of the key lessons we learned from this hard but transformative work. I don't have the room to give a comprehensive list of our lessons, but these were among the most critical.

Lesson One: Build the system to put the data in the hands of the classroom teacher. When presented clearly and consistently, data can empower teachers and provide them with the information necessary to drive academic results in their classrooms. To do this at Friendship, we needed to expand the amount of data available to these key end users in real time and organize the data set in a way that would allow teachers to interpret it in rapid and actionable ways.

With the help of an illustration, I'll describe what that looked like for us. We started with the premise that we didn't want to force our teachers to use two different software platforms. We already had student information systems in the classroom, which helped teachers track attendance, behavior, and grades on assignments. On top of this system we built a series of customized dashboards that allow teachers to do much more than they could previously.

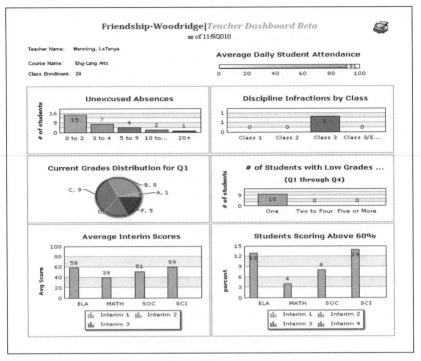

Figure 2: Friendship-Woodbridge Teacher Dashboard

Figure 2 shows a screen shot of a dashboard that gives teachers a real-time view into the average daily attendance, number of unexcused absences, low grades, and test scores, among other things. Each chart on the dashboard allows the teacher to "drill down" to the underlying data—or, as we put it, "move from numbers to names." Previously, our teachers had to compile data on Excel spreadsheets to get access in one place to all of their student indicators. Today, any time an entry is made in a student record, the dashboards update automatically—saving each teacher as much as eight hours a month.

I recently visited classrooms where teachers posted their dashboards as their classroom "scorecard" to motivate students to work together to improve attendance and reduce discipline infractions. In a fourth-grade class, students proudly showed me the day when they qualified for a pizza party by having thirty days in a row of no infractions and perfect attendance.

Lesson Two: Build the system to support teacher development, not just assessment. At Friendship, we've found that the best teachers are constantly learning and growing. In building our system we focused on collecting the data that would provide the information we needed in order to assess our teachers fairly and, as important, to nurture their growth.

The indicators on the teacher dashboards reflect the indicators chosen by teams of teachers, school leaders, parent representatives, and board members to be part of each teacher's performance evaluation and professional development planning. With performance indicators such as average daily attendance, discipline referrals, and student assessments, we are now putting in the hands of our teachers the data they would typically not have seen compiled until it was time for their evaluation. Each teacher now knows on a moment-to-moment basis how student performance in his or her classroom is tracking and can intervene more quickly and intelligently. Similarly, our coaches and administrators can see how each teacher is performing in order to build and deliver the professional development programs tailored to their specific needs.

We recently expanded one of our middle schools to serve early-childhood students, starting at preschool. Early in the school year, we brought the early-childhood teachers together to examine and discuss data on the young students. It was the first time that many of the teachers new to Friendship had ever had to share publicly how their students were performing against standards. "During the talk," the professional development organizer noted later, "our best teachers, especially from our established early-childhood programs, were able to help the new teachers around increasing vocabulary, improving instruction, and ensuring that early-childhood classrooms are more than just daycare."

Lesson Three: For real breakaway performance, make the data useful for students and parents (not just administrators and teachers). Friendship's overarching goal is to develop ethical, well-rounded, literate, and self-sufficient citizens. High student achievement, high graduation rates, and high levels of college acceptance are necessary but not sufficient results. College completion and career access are our higher aspirations. To achieve our goals for our students, we work to ensure that they develop the key behavioral competencies necessary for making good choices and that they demonstrate an independent drive for results outside the structured and supportive environment of our schools. Friendship's goals are expressed most clearly in our academic and extracurricular emphasis on parent and student ownership of individual performance.

Because of this emphasis, we built our performance-management system in a way that would ensure that students and their parents understand and value the new data. Teachers begin by helping students learn how to track their own data. We expect students as young as kindergartners to be able to explain and provide evidence of their progress to their teachers, their peers, and their parents. Once students have demonstrated sufficient mastery of these skills and behaviors, they are introduced to grade-level-appropriate student dashboard tools to assist them in tracking their progress and setting more ambitious goals for themselves. We extend our work to parents by preparing customized data reports that they can review with the teacher and their child. We've learned that our parents are hungry for more data about their child's progress and want to feel knowledgeable about what the data mean and what they can do to help their child succeed.

Worth the Investment

In today's environment of heightened accountability, it's easy to decide to institute a performance-management system, but it's not so easy to actually do it. For Friendship, the work has been challenging and is still ongoing. However, we have begun to be able to truly diagnose performance issues, better identify our best teachers, and better target solutions.

Our oldest and newest campuses best tell the story of the impact of building a system to better manage performance. At Chamberlain Elementary, which Friendship founded in 1998, we received our first standardized test results in the spring of 1999. We raised the percentage of proficient students to over 40 percent, but by 2006 proficiency languished in the mid to upper 30s. Since implementing the performance management system, we've seen a strong increase in reading and math proficiency. As seen in Figure 3, at our newest charter elementary campus, Southeast Elementary, our latest test scores show that we have more than doubled the proficient students in reading and math since opening the campus.

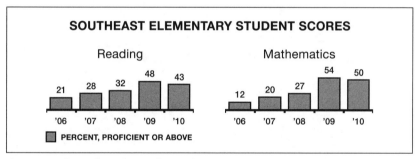

Figure 3: Southeast Elementary Proficiency Scores

"A" for Effort *and* Rigor

Prior to instituting our performance-management system, I often talked about J. Paul Getty's formula for success: "Rise early, work late, strike oil." I've now stopped using that quotation—and not because of people's associations with oil drilling in the aftermath of the BP disaster. The reason I've stopped using it is that I no longer want to give the impression that long hours are the most important factor in striking oil, or educating students. Nowadays, the oil industry invests tremendous effort in collecting and using data to guide every aspect of operations, and they get a huge return on that investment. That is what we are trying to do at Friendship. We want to know in real time where to invest time, energy, and money to move student achievement throughout the classroom, the schoolhouse, and the network of schools we manage.

A strong work ethic will always be key to our approach. But now we have the data to help us direct that effort in a way that more predictably produces student success.

An Integrated Approach to Outcomes Assessment

by Ethan D. Schafer, Ph.D.

———

Nonprofit and educational leaders often wish they had a simple tool-kit for determining whether their programs are working to improve the lives of those they serve. Unfortunately, no such silver bullet exists. Nor should it. The only way for schools and other organizations to get a full, useful sense of what's working and what's not is to invest significant time in developing an integrated, comprehensive approach. The organization can't just settle for information that's easy to measure. It must clarify what's *important* to measure and then determine how best to do so using both qualitative and quantitative means.

At the Lawrence School, an independent, private day school in Northeast Ohio serving students in grades one through twelve who learn differently, we are beginning to define desired outcomes for our students and gather data to determine what works (and what doesn't). We hope that these experiences will serve as a precursor to the development of an outcomes-driven performance framework. Although we are still in the early stages of this work and recognize that the outcomes we are defining are very specific to our school and its unique population, I believe that we're learning important lessons that are applicable to other organizations providing direct services to children and youth.

Beyond #2 Pencils

As a psychologist specializing in assessment, I spend much of my time reminding students, families, and educational leaders to consider what each kind of data truly measures and how much it matters for an individual or organization at that particular moment. We're learning that meaningful outcomes assessment requires flexibility; a clear focus on the right outcomes with measurement of each student's incremental gains; and dedication to observing the whole student. Accepting the level of ambiguity that comes with the progression of small steps toward achieving ultimate outcomes (e.g., a diploma) is necessary in these early stages.

Intelligent use of independent testing (e.g., standardized tests given to groups or individuals) is one critical component of outcomes assessment. Unfortunately, the hyper-polarized political climate regarding testing has obscured both the value and the limitations of standardized measurement methods and has triggered a holy war between "More testing!" on one side and "Get rid of all testing!" on the other.

But test data alone are insufficient in our work with students who learn differently. Looking at "functional outcomes" in combination with test scores provides a more complete picture of the developmental progress and impact we seek. Functional outcomes are the real-life variables that often matter most to a person or an organization. For example, consider these questions that speak to important functional outcomes:

○ If my child goes through your program, will she be more likely to graduate from high school and college?

○ Are youth from my program on a strong path to independent adulthood (i.e., less likely to be incarcerated, living on public assistance, or unemployed)?

- Can this student balance a checkbook, follow a budget, read a bus schedule?

Functional outcomes are often qualitative in nature, but this does not mean that such data should be considered "soft" or less valuable. Functional outcomes data provide critical evidence about the real-world impact of an intervention on a child's life, both in terms of change on a personal level (e.g., she reads more books) and the attainment of important milestones (e.g., she earns her bachelor's degree).

Determining which functional outcomes we are trying to effect, why we are trying to effect them, and how we can do so provides a framework within which we focus, communicate, and demonstrate our efforts. Determining critical functional outcomes is often as simple as rewording your organization's main goals, which might look something like this:

- I want our kids to stay in school longer.

- I want to reduce turnover within key organizational areas.

- I want our kids to keep a job for two years.

A good functional outcome is one that matters, is easy to see, and requires no special skill for understanding its relevance.

Outcomes Assessment in Action

At the Lawrence School, we use a multi-faceted approach to outcomes assessment. Lawrence students often arrive feeling defeated, deflated, and disappointed despite their valiant attempts to learn in a general-education environment that neither understood nor honored their unique approaches to problem solving. As a result, they enter the school with reading, writing, and math skills that are well below average.

Because our students learn differently, our approach to assessment varies in both structure and intent. We believe that the overall success of an individual student's development and our intervention strategies is best measured through frequent, standardized assessments combined with individualized attention.

We use tests, administered by trained professionals, that are intentionally *not* tied to our curriculum. Results therefore reflect a completely independent evaluation, in much the same way that a company's finances are audited by outside accountants. Each student is tested before admission and again at the end of the school year, and average and individual scores are tracked to identify programmatic and individual areas of need. Teacher observations and performance on daily class work are also factored equally into a student's progress evaluation, as are reports from parents about improvements in quality of life at home and in behavior at school.

Our integrated perspective helps trained teachers explain these data to parents *and* students in the context of curricular and functional domains so that the scores have appropriate meaning. Our careful approach to gathering data also provides opportunities for teachers to adjust their teaching strategies, integrate support, and otherwise personalize the delivery of curriculum.

Do We Do What We Say We Do?

At Lawrence, we focus on three areas—curriculum mastery, functional outcomes, and performance on scientifically developed standardized tests—which shift in relative importance as the student gets older. Preliminary results from tracking students in grades one through six show that, after three years, the average Lawrence student is indistinguishable from a typical student his or her age in basic reading, math, and writing skills. Note the conceptualization of the data: We see getting back into the *normal* range as an important outcome for children with learning differences, since a primary need involves addressing academic deficits. When we can tell parents that their child, who cried and fought to get out of school because he was so far behind his friends, is now reading like any other child his age, the emotional impact of our institutional goals is palpable.

By providing unambiguous evidence of improvement in basic academic skills, these data indicate a promising start and show that we are doing what we say we are doing. But it's a marathon, not a sprint. We will continue to follow each student to see if gains are maintained and to ensure that our efforts are yielding benefits as a program and for each individual student. Additionally, we must determine the relationship between gains on these tests and a student's progress in curriculum and functional domains so that the results can be integrated and communicated in an effective way that leads to positive changes (e.g., more efficient allocation of limited resources) in our organization. If our data cannot be used to help *both* individual students *and* the program as a whole, we are wasting our time.

Yet, using this integrated approach is not without obstacles. Not every organization has easy access to a psychologist or other professionals trained to administer tests individually. It takes considerable time and resources to record and track data; determine which functional outcomes to measure and how to measure them; and ascertain how the data will be used for the benefit of individual students and the program as a whole. But this is the exciting part. After all of this work, we are left with a plan that is real, not theoretical, and concrete ideas about how to do more of what's working and eliminate what's not.

Programmatic victories can't be claimed overnight. We are still working on how best to measure basic skill development in our Upper School students, since deficits in older children are more likely to be resistant to intervention and since testing in basic skills does not address the complex problem-solving and abstract-thinking abilities that are so critical. We also can't say definitively that Lawrence students are more likely to graduate from college, because there have been only six graduating classes; we need many more years of data. Still, we can say that Lawrence graduates attend two- and four-year colleges at a rate of about 96 percent, compared with 16 percent of children with learning differences who don't go to Lawrence. So, after several years of work, we can declare, "We have preliminary data indicating that we are succeeding, but we have a long way to go."

Conclusion

Vanessa Diffenbacher, head of Lawrence's Lower School, explains the underlying rationale for our integrated approach to outcomes assessment: "We want to teach our students the foundational skills of lifelong learning, not just passing the next test. We teach them how to become independent learners, not what to memorize, and no single test suffices for measuring that kind of progress. Our approach reflects our emphasis on the whole child and lets us know if we are succeeding both as a program and for each individual student. Yes, it's a huge amount of work for us, but our students deserve it."

An integrated approach to assessment helps us construct appropriate learning environments and develop instructional approaches and practices that make stepping stones out of stumbling blocks for both students and teachers. It requires a great deal of institutional courage to refuse to default to a one-size-fits-all, cookie-cutter view and instead to pursue meaningful measurement for each student, but we've found the payoff worthwhile. Perhaps Lou Salza, Lawrence head of school, put it best when he said, "Learning is a personal experience: one size fits few." Meaningful outcomes measurement follows that same maxim.

Contributors

―――

Patricia Brantley

Patricia Brantley is chief operating officer of Friendship Public Charter School, a $30 million local education agency serving eight thousand students. She is responsible for strategic initiatives, new school expansion, and oversight of existing school operations. She has launched a number of signature programs to extend the Friendship brand, including Supplemental Education Services, the Friendship News Network, and the Friendship Leadership Development Academy. She has also strengthened Friendship's development capacity, raising millions of dollars in new grants and donations. Before becoming COO, she facilitated the restructuring of Friendship's Collegiate Academy and the start-up of the first Early College High School in Washington, DC.

A graduate of Princeton University, Pat has served in a variety of corporate and nonprofit leadership positions, including founding director of the Partnership for Academic Achievement; vice president of Washington Linkage Group, a government relations and public affairs firm; interim executive director of the Dance Institute of Washington; chief development officer for the National Council of Negro Women; national manager of marketing and public relations for the Black Family Reunion; vice president of client services for Correct Communications; and manager of services marketing for Prudential Insurance Company. She is co-founder of the Catalyst Project, an initiative to foster innovation and accountable leadership in the civic sector.

Laura Callanan

Laura Callanan joined the Social Sector Office of McKinsey & Company in 2008 as a member of the Philanthropy Practice. She supports foundation and nonprofit clients, leads work on sustainable capitalism, and leads the Learning for Social Impact initiative (lsi.mckinsey.com).

Immediately prior to joining McKinsey, Laura was an independent consultant working with the Synergos Institute, a nonprofit organization addressing global poverty and social injustice, and E-Line Media, a double-bottom-line publisher of video games with social impact. Previously, she was senior advisor at the United Nations Development Programme in the Bureau for Crisis Prevention and Recovery, where she served as chief of staff, and executive director of the Prospect Hill Foundation, where she oversaw grantmaking in the areas of environmental conservation, reproductive health and rights, and nuclear nonproliferation.

Before that, she was an associate director at the Rockefeller Foundation. She had general management responsibility for all activities related to the $3 billion endowment and investment responsibility for the foundation's venture capital and private equity portfolio. She also served as a member of the foundation's Program Venture Experiment (ProVenEx) commitment committee and oversaw investment decisions for program-related investments and similar public-private activities. Laura is an adjunct professor at New York University's Stern School of Business, where she teaches about the nonprofit capital marketplace.

Isaac Castillo

Isaac Castillo is director of learning and evaluation for the Latin American Youth Center (LAYC) in Washington, DC. He oversees all of LAYC's research and evaluation efforts, including the implementation and maintenance of a center-wide database system to track demographic and outcomes information on all youth attending programs at LAYC. He also provides direct assistance to each LAYC program with the intent of improving outcomes and facilitating effective reporting to funding agencies. His work at LAYC has been highlighted in publications such as the *Chronicle of Philanthropy*, *Youth Today*, and the *Wall Street Journal*.

Prior to joining LAYC, Isaac worked with a private research and evaluation firm in Bethesda, MD, and completed program and cross-site evaluations for a wide spectrum of agencies, including federal and state governments, private foundations, and community-based organizations. In 2000 he completed an evaluation entitled "Assessment of State Minority Health Infrastructure and Capacity to Address Issues of Health Disparity" for the U.S. Office of Minority Health. He also worked on an evaluation designed to measure the effectiveness of school- and community-based violence-prevention programs for gang-involved youth, sponsored by the Office of Juvenile Justice and Delinquency Prevention.

Isaac received his undergraduate degree in human resource management from Syracuse University and his M.S. in public policy analysis from the University of Rochester. As an undergraduate Isaac was named an All-American Debater. He continues to work with the debate community, currently serving on the board of directors for the Associated Leaders of Urban Debate (ALOUD).

Carol Thompson Cole

Carol Thompson Cole is president and CEO of Venture Philanthropy Partners (VPP), a philanthropic-investment organization that helps great leaders build strong, high-performing nonprofit institutions.

Carol came to VPP with more than twenty years of management experience in the public and private sectors, as well as a strong history of leadership in the National Capital Region's nonprofit community and local government. She served as special advisor to President Clinton on the District of Columbia and executive director of the DC Inter-Agency Task Force, Executive Office of the President, where she was "point person" to the president on the District and played a key role in developing ways for the federal government to assist Washington, DC, in achieving and sustaining financial stability, reliable services, and economic growth.

Previously, she was vice president for government and environmental affairs at RJR Nabisco and spent twelve years holding major management and staff positions in the government of the District of Columbia, most notably as the first woman (and, at the time, the youngest person) to be appointed city administrator.

She is a member of the Greater Washington Advisory Board of SunTrust, the Kaiser Permanente Regional Advisory Board, and the Federal City Council. She serves on the board of trustees of Wesley Theological Seminary and the Summit Fund. She is vice chair of the Community Foundation for the National Capital Region and a lifetime trustee of the Urban Institute.

Carol earned a B.A. from Smith College and a master's degree in public administration with a concentration in urban public policy studies from the Robert F. Wagner School of Public Service, New York University. She also attended the Senior Executives in State and Local Government Program at Harvard University's Kennedy School of Government.

David E. K. Hunter, Ph.D.

Since September 2006, David E. K. Hunter has served as a consultant internationally to funders, ministries, and direct service agencies in the social (not-for-profit) and public sectors. He focuses on organizational capacity building; the development of strategies and theories of change; performance management; and the creation, delivery, and assessment of social value. His practice builds on more than three decades of experience using performance-management systems to improve the quality and effectiveness of social services. As superintendent of a state psychiatric hospital in Connecticut, he promoted improved hospital safety and lower patient length of stay while attaining better treatment outcomes. The changes led to the hospital's receiving Accreditation with Commendation from the Joint Commission on the Accreditation of Health Care Organizations.

Subsequently, at the Edna McConnell Clark Foundation, David helped nonprofit organizations develop clear value propositions through capacity-building "theory of change" workshops, and worked with them to design, implement, and use performance-management systems to deliver, monitor, learn from, and evaluate high-quality, effective, and efficient human services.

David is the author of numerous articles and papers about strategic performance management and how to create, invest in, and sustain social value in complex situations with diverse stakeholders. A founding member of the Alliance for Effective Social Investing, he co-authored the *Guide to Effective Social Investing*, published by the Alliance, and developed the web-based Social Investment Risk Assessment (SIRA) tool to help funders assess the potential social value of investing in a given nonprofit agency.

Jonathan Law

Jonathan Law is a consultant in McKinsey & Company's Social Sector Office in New York City. Since joining the firm in 2001, he has worked with senior clients in the social sector and in financial services. His client work has focused on social impact assessment, urban revitalization, and policy and advocacy. He recently helped lead the Learning for Social Impact initiative, a collaboration between McKinsey's Social Sector Office and top U.S. foundations and sector thought leaders.

Prior to joining McKinsey, Jonathan worked at the United Nations, the New York City Economic Development Corporation, and the law firm of Cravath, Swaine & Moore.

Jonathan earned an A.B. in social studies from Harvard College and a J.D. from Columbia Law School.

Kristin Anderson Moore, Ph.D.

Kristin Anderson Moore, a social psychologist, is a senior scholar and senior program area director for youth development at Child Trends. She has been with Child Trends since 1982, including fourteen years directing the organization before choosing to return to full-time research in 2006, studying trends in child and family well-being, the effects of family structure and social change on children, the determinants and consequences of adolescent parenthood, the effects of welfare and poverty on children, and positive development. Her nationally recognized expertise includes her work on the conceptualization of fatherhood, healthy marriage, and positive development for children and youth. She has contributed to numerous surveys, including the ECLS-B, the National Survey of Children's Health, the National Survey of Children, the National Survey of Children and Parents, the National Survey of America's Families, the National Survey of Family Growth, and the 1997 National Longitudinal Survey of Youth. She has also worked on numerous evaluations, including the National Evaluation of Welfare to Work Strategies and Pregnancy Prevention Approaches.

Kris was the founding chair of the Effective Programs and Research Task Force for the National Campaign to Prevent Teen and Unplanned Pregnancy and served as a member of its initial board of directors. She also served on the Advisory Council of the National Institute of Child Health and Human Development. In 1999 she received the Foundation for Child Development Centennial Award for linking research on children's development to policies that serve the public interest. The Society for Adolescent Medicine selected her as the 2002 SAM Visiting Professor in Adolescent Research, and she received the 2005 Distinguished Contribution Award from the American Sociological Association's section on Children and Youth. In 2010 she was named Researcher of the Year by the Healthy Teen Network.

She currently serves on advisory boards for the Edna McConnell Clark Foundation, Big Brothers Big Sisters, WINGS for Kids, First Place for Youth, and the Family Impact Seminar. Kris received her Ph.D. in social psychology from the University of Michigan.

Mario Morino

Mario Morino is co-founder and chairman of Venture Philanthropy Partners (VPP) and chairman of the Morino Institute. His career spans more than forty-five years as entrepreneur, technologist, and civic and business leader. He also has a long history of civic engagement and philanthropy in the National Capital Region and Northeast Ohio.

In the early 1970s, Mario co-founded and helped build the LEGENT Corporation, a software and services firm that became a market leader and one of the industry's ten largest firms by the early 1990s. He retired from the private sector in 1992. Since then, he has sought to level the playing field for children of low-income families, focusing almost exclusively on economic, social, and educational issues.

Mario founded the Morino Institute in 1994 to stimulate innovation and entrepreneurship, advance a more effective philanthropy, close social divides, and understand the impact of the Internet on our society. In 2000 Mario co-founded VPP as a philanthropic-investment organization that concentrates investments of money, expertise, and contacts to improve the lives and boost the opportunities of children of low-income families in the National Capital Region. In 2010 VPP was one of only eleven organizations selected by the Social Innovation Fund, administered by the Corporation for National and Community Service, for its inaugural portfolio.

In addition to his roles with VPP and the Morino Institute, Mario serves as a member of the board of trustees of the Cleveland Clinic Foundation, an honorary trustee of the Brookings Institution, an emeritus trustee of Case Western Reserve University, a board member of the Lawrence School, and a board member of Saint Joseph Academy. He is a special advisor to Echoing Green and Within3; a member of the PEACE X PEACE advisory council; a member of the advisory board for the Center for the Advancement of Social Entrepreneurship (CASE), Fuqua School of Business, Duke University; and a member of the board of governors of the Partnership for Public Service. He also informally advises scores of organizations and individuals across a range of areas.

He lives in Greater Cleveland with his wife and three children.

David Murphey, Ph.D.

David Murphey is a senior research scientist at Child Trends with expertise in selecting, developing, monitoring, and analyzing indicators of child and youth well-being at the national, state, and local levels. He manages Child Trends' DataBank, an online compendium of more than one hundred indicators of child and family well-being, and provides technical assistance to state KIDS COUNT grantees and other projects involving place-based well-being initiatives.

Previously, David was senior policy analyst in the Planning Division, Vermont Agency of Human Services, where he was responsible for managing the collection of social indicators statewide, reporting on the collection, and preparing Vermont's *Community Profiles*—local reports on social indicators for the state's sixty school districts. He was instrumental in developing indicators for Vermont in the emerging areas of civic engagement, school readiness, and positive youth development, and provided technical assistance around indicator use for a variety of community and state partners. He holds a master's degree in education and a Ph.D. in developmental psychology, both from the University of Michigan.

Tynesia Boyea Robinson

Tynesia Boyea Robinson is the executive director of Year Up, National Capital Region, a nonprofit committed to providing significant growth opportunities for underserved young adults. Her wide range of experiences in information technology, Six Sigma, and international business development make her a valuable asset to the Year Up team. She has led growth from a class of twenty-two students and eight corporate partners in 2006 to a class of nearly five hundred students and more than three hundred corporate partners in 2009. A performance-assessment tool that she created for Year Up was recognized by the Bridgespan Group as an industry best practice.

Prior to joining Year Up, Tynesia held leadership roles in several business units at General Electric. She was responsible for integrating processes, policies, and more than two hundred employees into GE Mortgage Insurance. Earlier in her career, she led several eBusiness and process-improvement projects at GE Transportation Systems. In addition to her work responsibilities, Tynesia was the community service chair for the GE African American Forum and a mentor to young adults through various community and faith-based groups.

Tynesia, who holds a dual degree in electrical engineering and computer science from Duke University, received her MBA from Harvard Business School, where she won the Harvard Student Association MBA Award, played the lead in their annual musical satire, and was a founding member of the HBS student group Business Plan for Black America (BPBA), commissioned by the NAACP to improve education, economics, and opportunities for disadvantaged African Americans.

Ethan D. Schafer, Ph.D.

Ethan D. Schafer is a licensed child clinical psychologist. He is an adjunct assistant professor in the Department of Psychology at Case Western Reserve University, where he teaches graduate courses on psychological assessment of children, clinical supervision, and consulting. He is the consulting psychologist and assessment center director at the Lawrence School, an independent, coeducational K-12 school for children who learn differently. At Lawrence, Ethan consults with families to ensure that their students' mental health needs are met, coordinates services with local providers, and provides strategies to faculty and staff to help them work more effectively with vulnerable students. He also supervises doctoral students' training at the Assessment Center, which provides high-quality, low-cost psychological and learning evaluations to families in Northeast Ohio. He directs Lawrence's comprehensive outcomes effort, which evaluates the success of the program as well as individual students through the systematic collection and analysis of good outcomes data.

Finally, Ethan maintains a private practice and consulting business, specializing in the treatment of anxiety and mood disorders in adolescents and consulting with summer camps and schools across the country. He graduated Phi Beta Kappa with high honors in psychology from the University of Michigan in 1998 and earned his doctorate in clinical child psychology at Case Western Reserve University in 2004. He lives with his wife and son in Greater Cleveland.

Lynn Taliento

Lynn Taliento is a partner at McKinsey & Company. Based in Washington, DC, she played a founding role in the creation of the firm's Social Sector Office (SSO), which brings an objective, fact-based approach leading to tailored solutions to complex societal challenges. The SSO has specific expertise in economic development, global public health, education, and strategic philanthropy.

Lynn works exclusively with national and international foundations, nonprofit organizations, and individual philanthropists on issues of strategy, organization, and operations. She has particular expertise in the areas of advocacy, strategic planning, private-public partnerships, and governance. Her recent work includes developing a strategy for an innovative advocacy effort focused on global poverty, defining a five-year plan for one of the largest international development organizations in the world, analyzing impact and best practices in the field, and creating an advocacy strategy for a leading foundation.

Fluent in Spanish, Lynn spent four years in McKinsey's Mexico City office, where she worked on strategy and policy engagements for clients in the public, private, and nonprofit sectors. Prior to joining McKinsey in 1994, she was an advisor to the minister of the economy of the Czech Republic and a press secretary in the U.S. House of Representatives.

Lynn graduated *summa cum laude* from Yale University with a bachelor's degree in American Studies, and she earned a master's degree in public policy from the John F. Kennedy School of Government at Harvard University, where she was a Kennedy Fellow. She lives in Washington, DC, with her husband and two children.

Karen Walker, Ph.D.

Karen Walker is a senior research scientist at Child Trends. She is a sociologist with broad expertise in evaluation research on programs that support child and adolescent development, with a particular emphasis on after-school and other youth development programs. Throughout her career, she has conducted a broad range of multi-method, multi-disciplinary research projects, pairing outcomes studies with rigorous implementation studies that help explain outcomes and describe the organizational, programmatic, policy, and cultural processes and climates in which programs operate.

Karen focuses extensively on evaluations of community initiatives that forge partnerships within communities, including the Children's Futures initiative, an early-childhood initiative in Trenton, NJ; the San Francisco Beacon initiative, youth development centers established by a public-private partnership in San Francisco; Plain Talk, an initiative to prevent teen pregnancy; and the Extended-Service Schools Initiative, an evaluation of the seventeen-city Wallace Funds demonstration of four models of after-school programs.

Prior to coming to Child Trends, Karen was a research professor in the Psychology Department at the University of Virginia and vice president for research at Public/Private Ventures.

EDITORS

Lowell Weiss

Lowell Weiss is president of Cascade Philanthropy Advisors, which provides personalized guidance to a wide range of foundations and individual donors seeking to deepen their impact. Previously, he served in a leadership role at the Bill & Melinda Gates Foundation. Among his many responsibilities, he served as staff director of the internal team responsible for providing Bill and Melinda Gates with analytical insights on how to make the highest and best use of Warren Buffett's historic gift to the foundation. Prior to joining the Gates Foundation, he served as director of the chairman's office at the Morino Institute, which is dedicated to improving the lives of at-risk children in the National Capital Region.

As special assistant to the president in the Clinton White House, Lowell traveled extensively with the president, wrote more than 150 speeches for him, and served as a key communications strategist on issues ranging from the environment to economic development. He wrote a *New York Times* bestselling book with political consultant James Carville; served as an editor at the *Atlantic Monthly*; and published articles in magazines including the *Atlantic Monthly*, *U.S. News & World Report*, and the *New Republic*.

He serves on the board of City Year Seattle/King County, is a partner of Social Venture Partners Seattle, and recently led a successful grassroots campaign in Washington State to strengthen laws on cellphone use while driving. He graduated *magna cum laude* from Amherst College. He lives in Seattle with his wife and their two children.

Cheryl Collins

Cheryl Collins is senior advisor for Morino Ventures, LLC. She began working with Mario Morino in October 1992, during his "discovery/ journey" phase that led to the Morino Institute's formation in 1994. Since then, she has served in key behind-the-scenes roles and provided support to philanthropic, educational, and civic initiatives of the Morino Institute and family, including the Potomac KnowledgeWay Project, the Netpreneur Program, the Youth Development Collaborative (YDC) Pilot, the YouthLearn Initiative, and Venture Philanthropy Partners. She administers the Morino Institute grant program and the Morino family's scholars program, which provides student scholarships at several colleges and universities. Her operations roles have encompassed a diverse set of responsibilities, including technology management, editorial oversight, web production, knowledge management, and research. Previously, Cheryl worked with students in grades seven through twelve, teaching English, journalism, and creative writing, and she was a program advisor for gifted programs at the Arkansas Department of Education.

An active volunteer for her community of faith, she has worked with the preschool program since 1994 and serves on Southview Community Church's personnel committee. Cheryl received a B.A. from Hendrix College, an M.Ed. in administration from Harding University, and an M.Ed. in gifted and talented education from the University of Arkansas at Little Rock. She lives in Northern Virginia.